DALAI LAMA
(TENZIN GYATSO)

SPIRITUAL LEADERS AND THINKERS

MARY BAKER EDDY

MOHANDAS GANDHI

AYATOLLAH RUHOLLAH KHOMEINI

MARTIN LUTHER

AIMEE SEMPLE McPHERSON

THOMAS MERTON

DALAI LAMA (TENZIN GYATSO)

SPIRITUAL
LEADERS AND
THINKERS

DALAI LAMA
(TENZIN GYATSO)

Richard Worth

Introductory Essay by
Martin E. Marty, Professor Emeritus
University of Chicago Divinity School

CHELSEA HOUSE
PUBLISHERS
A Haights Cross Communications Company

Philadelphia

FRONTIS   After being forced to flee his native Tibet, the Fourteenth Dalai Lama took refuge in Dharamsala, India. Today, the Dalai Lama remains exiled in India, while China claims Tibet as part of the Chinese nation.

CHELSEA HOUSE PUBLISHERS

VP, NEW PRODUCT DEVELOPMENT   Sally Cheney
DIRECTOR OF PRODUCTION   Kim Shinners
CREATIVE MANAGER   Takeshi Takahashi
MANUFACTURING MANAGER   Diann Grasse

Staff for DALAI LAMA (TENZIN GYATSO)

EXECUTIVE EDITOR   Lee Marcott
SENIOR EDITOR   Tara Koellhoffer
PRODUCTION EDITOR   Megan Emery
ASSISTANT PHOTO EDITOR   Noelle Nardone
SERIES AND COVER DESIGNER   Keith Trego
LAYOUT   21st Century Publishing and Communications, Inc.

A Haights Cross Communications ⌐ Company

www.chelseahouse.com

First Printing

9 8 7 6 5 4 3 2 1

Library of Congress Cataloging-in-Publication Data applied for.

ISBN 0-7910-7868-X

CONTENTS

Foreword

Why become acquainted with notable people when making efforts to understand the religions of the world?

Most of the faith communities number hundreds of millions of people. What can attention paid to one tell about more, if not most, to say nothing of *all*, their adherents? Here is why:

The people in this series are exemplars. If you permit me to take a little detour through medieval dictionaries, their role will become clear.

In medieval lexicons, the word *exemplum* regularly showed up with a peculiar definition. No one needs to know Latin to see that it relates to "example" and "exemplary." But back then, *exemplum* could mean something very special.

That "ex-" at the beginning of such words signals "taking out" or "cutting out" something or other. Think of to "excise" something, which is to snip it out. So, in the more interesting dictionaries, an *exemplum* was referred to as "a clearing in the woods," something cut out of the forests.

These religious figures are *exempla*, figurative clearings in the woods of life. These clearings and these people perform three functions:

First, they define. You can be lost in the darkness, walking under the leafy canopy, above the undergrowth, plotless in the pathless forest. Then you come to a clearing. It defines with a sharp line: there, the woods end; here, the open space begins.

Great religious figures are often stumblers in the dark woods.

We see them emerging in the bright light of the clearing, blinking, admitting that they had often been lost in the mysteries of existence, tangled up with the questions that plague us all, wandering without definition. Then they discover the clearing, and, having done so, they point our way to it. We then learn more of who we are and where we are. Then we can set our own direction.

Second, the *exemplum*, the clearing in the woods of life, makes possible a brighter vision. Great religious pioneers in every case experience illumination and then they reflect their light into the hearts and minds of others. In Buddhism, a key word is *enlightenment*. In the Bible, "the people who walked in darkness have seen a great light." They see it because their prophets or savior brought them to the sun in the clearing.

Finally, when you picture a clearing in the woods, an *exemplum*, you are likely to see it as a place of cultivation. Whether in the Black Forest of Germany, on the American frontier, or in the rain forests of Brazil, the clearing is the place where, with light and civilization, residents can cultivate, can produce culture. As an American moviegoer, my mind's eye remembers cinematic scenes of frontier days and places that pioneers hacked out of the woods. There, they removed stones, planted, built a cabin, made love and produced families, smoked their meat, hung out laundered clothes, and read books. All that can happen in clearings.

In the case of these religious figures, planting and cultivating and harvesting are tasks in which they set an example and then inspire or ask us to follow. Most of us would not have the faintest idea how to find or be found by God, to nurture the Holy Spirit, to create a philosophy of life without guidance. It is not likely that most of us would be satisfied with our search if we only consulted books of dogma or philosophy, though such may come to have their place in the clearing.

Philosopher Søren Kierkegaard properly pointed out that you cannot learn to swim by being suspended from the ceiling on a belt and reading a "How To" book on swimming. You learn because a parent or an instructor plunges you into water, supports you when necessary, teaches you breathing and motion, and then releases you to swim on your own.

Kierkegaard was not criticizing the use of books. I certainly have nothing against books. If I did, I would not be commending this series to you, as I am doing here. For guidance and courage in the spiritual quest, or—and this is by no means unimportant!—in intellectual pursuits, involving efforts to understand the paths others have taken, there seems to be no better way than to follow a fellow mortal, but a man or woman of genius, depth, and daring. We "see" them through books like these.

Exemplars come in very different styles and forms. They bring differing kinds of illumination, and then suggest or describe diverse patterns of action to those who join them. In the case of the present series, it is possible for someone to repudiate or disagree with *all* the religious leaders in this series. It is possible also to be nonreligious and antireligious and therefore to disregard the truth claims of all of them. It is more difficult, however, to ignore them. Atheists, agnostics, adherents, believers, and fanatics alike live in cultures that are different for the presence of these people. "Leaders and thinkers" they may be, but most of us do best to appraise their thought in the context of the lives they lead or have led.

If it is possible to reject them all, it is impossible to affirm everything that all of them were about. They disagree with each other, often in basic ways. Sometimes they develop their positions and ways of thinking by separating themselves from all the others. If they met each other, they would likely judge each other cruelly. Yet the lives of each and all of them make a contribution to the intellectual and spiritual quests of those who go in ways other than theirs. There are tens of thousands of religions in the world, and millions of faith communities. Every one of them has been shaped by founders and interpreters, agents of change and prophets of doom or promise. It may seem arbitrary to walk down a bookshelf and let a finger fall on one or another, almost accidentally. This series may certainly look arbitrary in this way. Why precisely the choice of these exemplars?

In some cases, it is clear that the publishers have chosen someone who has a constituency. Many of the world's 54 million Lutherans may be curious about where they got their name, who the man Martin Luther was. Others are members of a community but choose isolation: The hermit monk Thomas Merton is typical. Still others are exiled and achieve their work far from the clearing in which they grew up; here the Dalai Lama is representative. Quite a number of the selected leaders had been made unwelcome, or felt unwelcome in the clearings, in their own childhoods and youth. This reality has almost always been the case with women like Mary Baker Eddy or Aimee Semple McPherson. Some are extremely controversial: Ayatollah Ruhollah Khomeini stands out. Yet to read of this life and thought as one can in this series will be illuminating in much of the world of conflict today.

Reading of religious leaders can be a defensive act: Study the lives of certain ones among them and you can ward off spiritual—and sometimes even militant—assaults by people who follow them. Reading and learning can be a personally positive act: Most of these figures led lives that we can indeed call exemplary. Such lives can throw light on communities of people who are in no way tempted to follow them. I am not likely to be drawn to the hermit life, will not give up my allegiance to medical doctors, or be successfully nonviolent. Yet Thomas Merton reaches me and many non-Catholics in our communities; Mary Baker Eddy reminds others that there are more ways than one to approach healing; Mohandas Gandhi stings the conscience of people in cultures like ours where resorting to violence is too frequent, too easy.

Finally, reading these lives tells something about how history is made by imperfect beings. None of these subjects is a god, though some of them claimed that they had special access to the divine, or that they were like windows that provided for illumination to that which is eternal. Most of their stories began with inauspicious childhoods. Sometimes they were victimized, by parents or by leaders of religions from which they later broke.

Some of them were unpleasant and abrasive. They could be ungracious toward those who were near them and impatient with laggards. If their lives were symbolic clearings, places for light, many of them also knew clouds and shadows and the fall of night. How they met the challenges of life and led others to face them is central to the plot of all of them.

I have often used a rather unexciting concept to describe what I look for in books: *interestingness*. The authors of these books, one might say, had it easy, because the characters they treat are themselves so interesting. But the authors also had to be interesting and responsible. If, as they wrote, they would have dulled the personalities of their bright characters, that would have been a flaw as marring as if they had treated their subjects without combining fairness and criticism, affection and distance. To my eye, and I hope in yours, they take us to spiritual and intellectual clearings that are so needed in our dark times.

Martin E. Marty
The University of Chicago

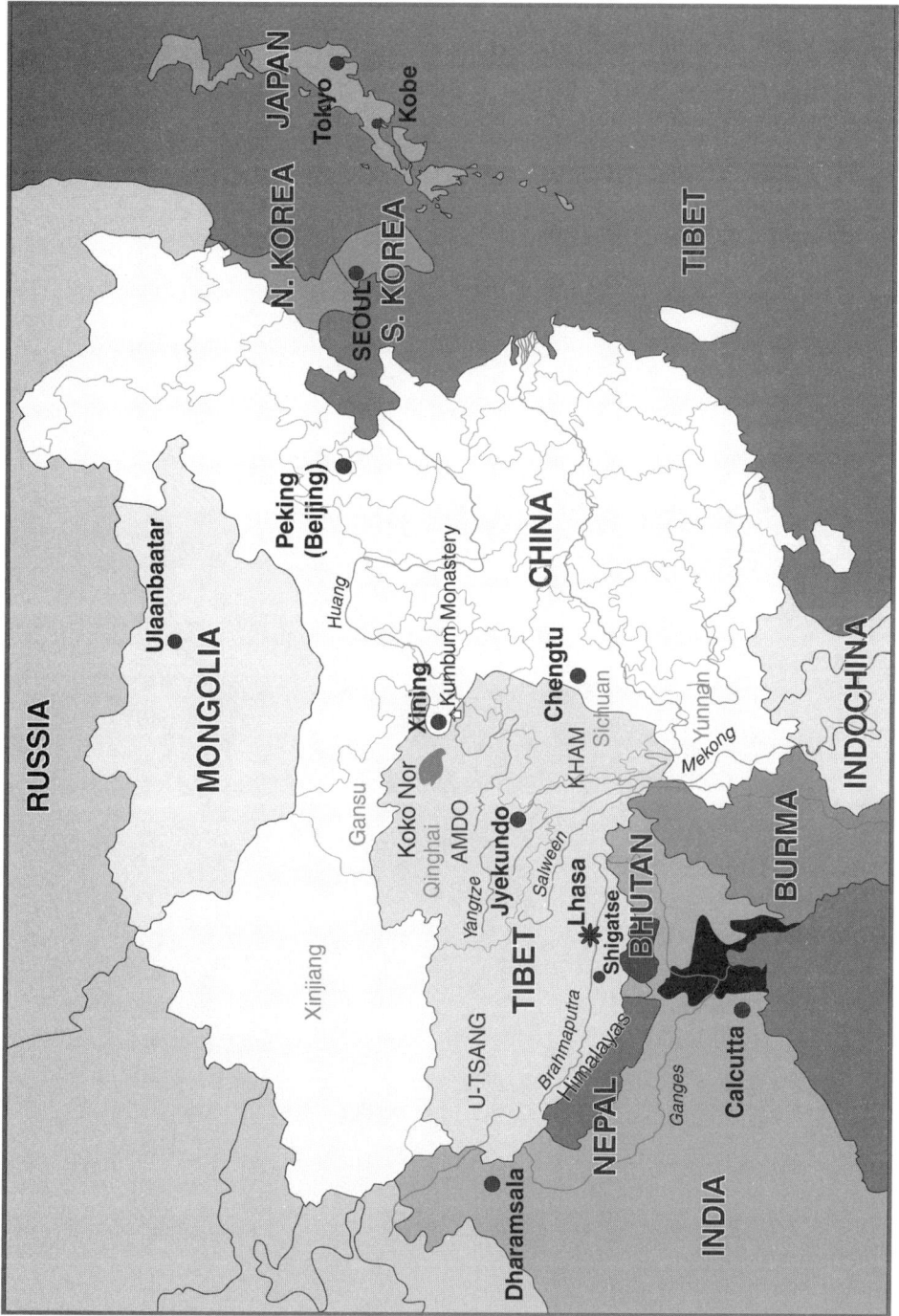

1

The Fourteenth Dalai Lama

To me "Dalai Lama" is a title
that signifies the office I hold.
I myself am just a human being,
and incidentally a Tibetan,
who chooses to be a Buddhist monk.

—Tenzin Gyatso, the Fourteenth Dalai Lama

In 1935, an unusual search began across the snow-covered mountains of Tibet. Two years earlier, the Great Thirteenth Dalai Lama had died. The search was on to find a new one.

In Tibet, the Dalai Lama is the religious and political leader of the country. The term *Dalai Lama* means "Great Ocean Teacher." Tibetan Buddhists believe that, after each Dalai Lama dies, he is reborn, or reincarnated, in his successor. The new Dalai Lama is a child who must be discovered so that he can be proclaimed as the spiritual leader of Tibetan Buddhism. In the meantime, a regent or temporary leader is appointed to run the government.

The 1935 search for the new Dalai Lama was begun by the regent with the help of other *lamas*—that is, teachers or monks. The searchers traveled to the lake of Lhamoi Lhatso, where people had claimed to see visions in the past. This lake was sacred to a great water god in Tibetan Buddhism.

After the lamas arrived at Lhamoi Lhatso, they gazed into the blue waters of the lake. Suddenly, they later recounted, a hole appeared in the lake's center and clouds settled above the hole. Within the hole, the lamas began to see visions. They saw a Buddhist monastery—a religious house where monks live. They also saw a small house with a blue roof, a peach tree with colorful flowers, a spotted dog, and the Tibetan letters *Ah, Ka,* and *Ma.*

The lamas believed that the vision was pointing them to the northeastern part of the country. The letter *Ah* seemed to stand for Amdo Province. So, early in 1936, a search party set out in that direction, led by a lama named Kewtsang Rinpoché.

It was a difficult journey. Tibet is perched in an area that has been called "the roof of the world." Much of the country is covered by the massive Himalayan and Kunlun mountains. Travelers must make their way along narrow roads and footpaths and up mountainsides to high plateaus. Snow falls during a large part of the year, making travel even more difficult. Indeed, Tibet is known as the Land of Snows.

Eventually, the search team arrived at the home of the Panchen Lama. This man is considered the second most important spiritual leader in Tibet. The Panchen Lama assured the searchers that they were on the right track. He even mentioned the names of three children whom he believed might be the next Dalai Lama. The searchers followed his advice and sought out the three boys. As it turned out, one of these boys had already died, and the second was disqualified because of his inappropriate behavior. By the time the searchers had learned this much, it was already 1937.

The team of lamas finally reached the town of Taktser on the northeastern Tibetan plateau. It was a tiny village with only a few houses, located at an elevation of about ten thousand feet. The people of Taktser lived in simple homes with flat roofs. The lamas immediately noticed, however, that the eaves (the section that overhangs the ends of the roof) were made of blue tiles, as they had seen in the vision at Lhamoi Lhatso. Nearby was the monastery of Kumbum, also seen in the vision. There was even one other connection: Many years earlier, the Great Thirteenth Dalai Lama had stopped near Taktser. Residents of the area believed he would someday return.

When the lamas arrived at the village, it was still winter. Approximately four feet of snow had fallen and the villagers were busy trying to remove it so they could walk outside. The lamas found a house that had a flowering peach tree on its property, which was unusual at that time of the year. The leader of the search team, high lama Kewtsang Rinpoché, disguised himself as a servant. He entered the house and began to talk with the people inside. Then he went into the kitchen, where he spoke with a three-year-old boy named Lhamo Dhondup (Thondup), whose name means "Wish-Fulfilling Goddess." The boy immediately recognized him as a high lama. Strangely, Lhamo Dhondup spoke in a Tibetan language that would not normally have been used by a child in Taktser.

Kewtsang Rinpoché then showed the boy some rosary beads, and Lhamo Dhondup claimed that he owned them. In fact, the rosary had earlier belonged to the late Thirteenth Dalai Lama. Later, the boy was shown various canes and other items, some of which had been owned by the Thirteenth Dalai Lama and some that had not. He consistently selected those items that had been the possessions of the Dalai Lama. Author Claude Levenson wrote:

> There was only one moment of hesitation in which it seemed he might make an error—after picking up a well-used cane, he examined it closely and then changed his mind, exchanging it for another one which was known by the examiners to have belonged to the thirteenth Dalai Lama. Yet his particular hesitation only reinforced the examiners' certainty of the identity of the child, for it turned out that the first cane he had selected had in fact originally belonged to the previous Dalai Lama, but that he had long ago made a present of it to one of his faithful servants.[1]

When Kewtsang Rinpoché prepared to leave, the boy announced that he wanted to go, too. He expected to be taken to Lhasa, the capital of Tibet.

The examiners were convinced that they had found the Fourteenth Dalai Lama. But they faced a serious problem. This area of Tibet was controlled by the Chinese. The local governor, Ma Pu-fang, was a greedy man. He demanded that the lamas hand over a bribe of about $90,000 or he would not let the child—or the Buddhist monks—leave the area.

While the monks tried to raise the money, Lhamo Dhondup was taken from his home and brought to the monastery at Kumbum. This large building was quite a change from the house where the child had grown up. Indeed, his entire life was suddenly changing.

Lhamo Dhondup's parents were small farmers who grew barley and potatoes. Barley combined with milk or tea becomes a common Tibetan food called *tsampa*. The family kept cows for milk and cheese as well as chickens, sheep, and yaks (shaggy-haired oxen). Yak butter is used in Tibetan tea. As the Dalai Lama later recalled: "I loved to follow my mother when she went to get eggs from the chicken coop. I would stay there and amuse myself with the chickens, it was so nice and warm in the straw. The house where I was born . . . was filled with a loving family atmosphere, though our conditions of life were humble, like all farmers then."[2]

When the money was finally raised to pay off the Chinese

governor, he was not satisfied. Instead, he now demanded three times the amount originally requested before he would allow the lamas to leave the area. Eventually, a group of traveling merchants agreed to loan them the money.

MOTHER OF THE DALAI LAMA

Diki Tsering, the mother of the Fourteenth Dalai Lama, was born in Amdo in 1901. The birth of a girl was not a reason for rejoicing in a Tibetan family at the start of the twentieth century. Boys were more important because they worked in the fields, planting and harvesting crops. In addition, a family had to provide a girl with a dowry—money paid to the parents of the groom—when she was married, so it could be expensive to raise a daughter.

Girls were not sent to school. Instead, they learned how to cook, sew, and clean the house. "Kitchens were the pride of every housewife," Diki Tsering wrote:

> They were very large, with walls constructed of stone. The cooking surface was a long stone, sometimes as long as eight to ten feet, with five to eight cooking holes in it. Through a large hole in the side the stove was filled with dried goat manure as fuel, and the fuel was lit through this hole. Every evening three large containers of fuel were put in. The next morning we bake one of our traditional breads, called *kunguntze.**

Diki Tsering was married when she was sixteen. The marriage had been arranged by her parents. In preparation for the wedding, she was given a large trousseau. It included clothes, jewelry, and thirty-five pair of shoes. Then she went to live in her new husband's home.

Beginning in 1919, she had four children before giving birth to the future Dalai Lama. "Lhamo Dhondup was different from my other children right from the start," she said. He was a somber child who liked to stay indoors by himself. He was always packing his clothes and his belongings. "When I asked what he was doing, he would reply that he was packing to go to Lhasa and would take all of us with him." Lhasa was the capital of Tibet and the home of the Dalai Lama.**

* Source: Diki Tsering, *Dalai Lama, My Son,* New York: Penguin Putnam, 2000, p. 37.

** Source: Ibid., p. 89.

By July 1939, the new Dalai Lama's caravan to Lhasa was ready to leave. The traveling party included the boy's brothers and parents. Lhamo Dhondup was carried on a splendid enclosed chair, called a *palanquin*, which was tied to the backs of two mules. The palanquin was decorated in yellow and had small windows. No one told the people along the way that Lhamo Dhondup was the Fourteenth Dalai Lama. They were still traveling through territory claimed by China, and they feared the Chinese might try to capture the new Dalai Lama. After three months of traveling, the caravan finally approached Lhasa and was met by a group of ambassadors from the government in the capital. Lhamo Dhondup was presented with a special white shawl, a *khata*. A proclamation was read announcing that he was the Fourteenth Dalai Lama. Then he was given numerous gifts.

As Dalai Lama biographers Roger Hicks and Ngakpa Chogyam wrote: "Everyone who remembers that occasion remarks on the way in which the little boy behaved. He received everyone as if it was the most natural thing in the world, dispensing blessings with perfect calm . . . despite the fact that he was only just over four years old and had never had any experience of court life."[3] The new Dalai Lama sat in a magnificent yellow tent, called the Peacock Tent, with other colorful tents nearby.

Late in 1939, he was carried into Lhasa. The city thronged with many thousands of inhabitants hoping to catch a glimpse of the new Dalai Lama. They cried out: "The sun of our happiness is risen!"[4] The boy was later taken to the Winter Palace, where he formally became the Fourteenth Dalai Lama. He was entertained by music and dancing. Musicians played large horns, bells, and cymbals.

During the festivities, he sat upon the traditional Lion Throne of Tibet. This large wooden chair, painted in gold with eight lions, had been a symbol of power for the past leaders of Tibet. Like his predecessors, the Fourteenth Dalai Lama took on the name of the Second Dalai Lama—*Gyatso*, which means "Ocean." From this time on, Lhamo Dhondup would be known as Tenzin Gyatso, "Great Ocean."

2

History of the Dalai Lamas

My doctrine is not a doctrine but just a vision.
I have not given you any set rules,
I have not given you a system.

—The Buddha

The story of Tibet's Buddhist leaders, the Dalai Lamas, begins with King Songtsen Gampo, who ruled during the seventh century. Songtsen Gampo was a highly successful military commander who built a great empire that included parts of India, China, and Mongolia. According to Tibetan history, Songtsen Gampo married the daughter of the king of Nepal and later married the daughter of the emperor of China. Both of these women were Buddhists. Tibetan tradition holds that Songtsen Gampo honored his wives by building each of them a Buddhist temple. One of these was the Jokhang Temple in Lhasa, considered the most important holy place for Tibetan Buddhism. The king also converted to the Buddhist religion and constructed many other temples throughout Tibet.

Buddhism was founded in India by Siddhartha Gautama during the sixth century B.C. A wealthy prince from Nepal, Siddhartha gave up his riches to wander the world seeking enlightenment. After he successfully discovered enlightenment in India during the 580s B.C., he took on the title *Buddha*. This means "one who has found enlightenment." After he became a Buddha, Siddhartha Gautama spread his beliefs and won many followers. His teachings were set down in writing, so they could continue to be studied by future generations. The original Buddhist teachings were written in Sanskrit, an ancient Indian language. In the seventh century, Tibetan scholars traveled to India, sent by King Songtsen Gampo, to translate the great Buddhist texts so they could be read in Tibet.

Tibetans believe that the Dalai Lama was incarnated—that is, lived—as Songtsen Gampo in a former life. They also believe that the Dalai Lama was incarnated as another great Tibetan king, Trisong Dretsen, who ruled during the eighth century. Trisong Dretsen's teacher was a Buddhist monk named Guru Rinpoché. A guru is a personal spiritual teacher. During the late eighth century, the king and Guru Rinpoché built the Samye Monastery—the first to be constructed in Tibet.

Trisong Dretsen was also a great military leader who enlarged the Tibetan Empire, capturing large parts of China. Buddhist monks from both China and India traveled to Tibet and studied at the religious centers that had been established in the country.

TIBETAN SAGES

Tibetan Buddhists believe that the Dalai Lamas have been incarnated as early sages, or learned men. (The word *lama* simply means "monk.") One of these early lamas was Dromtonpa, a great religious teacher who lived during the eleventh century. The Buddha himself had predicted Dromtonpa's coming when he wrote:

> *At the end of a five hundred year cycle [of my teaching]*
> *A layman will appear in the northern Land of Snows*
> *Who will bring great benefits to my enlightenment tradition. . . .*[5]

Lama Dromtonpa built Reting Monastery, an important center of Tibetan Buddhism.

Another great sage was Chogyal Phakpa, who was born in 1235. By this time, the Mongols had established the most powerful empire in Asia. Led by Genghis Khan, large forces of Mongol cavalry conquered vast territories that stretched from China into Persia. One of Genghis Khan's successors was his grandson Kublai Khan, who ruled the Mongolian Empire from his capital in Chengdu, China. Kublai Khan was converted to Buddhism by Chogyal Phakpa. According to historian Glenn Mullin, this was the beginning of the special relationship between Tibet and the Mongolian Khans. Because of Kublai Khan's sympathy for Tibet's Buddhist culture, Tibet remained independent, but under the protection of the powerful Mongolian Empire.[6]

FIRST DALAI LAMA

According to Tibetan beliefs, the first Dalai Lama was born in 1391. His parents were poor farmers who were attacked by robbers soon after their son's birth. His mother hid the baby in some rocks, so the robbers would not find him. When she came back to claim her son, she found a black bird, a raven, guarding him, so other birds would not peck him to death. At age seven, the boy was sent to a monastery where his uncle lived as a Buddhist monk. The boy excelled in his study of religious teachings, and he learned to become a highly skilled debater in Buddhist ideas. About 1411, he became an ordained monk, known as Gedun Drubpa, or "one who desires virtuous ends."

While in his twenties, Gedun Drubpa met Tsongkhapa—known in Tibetan history as Tsongkhapa the Great—who became his teacher. Tsongkhapa was the founder of the Gelugpa School of Tibetan Buddhism from which all the Dalai Lamas come. Other schools include Karmapa, Sakyapa, Brugpa, and Nyingmapa. The Gelugpa School was the most important, and its members were called Yellow Hats for the color of the caps the monks wore.

When he was in his thirties, Gedun Drubpa became a famous teacher. As early biographer Kunga Gyaltsen described him: "Whenever he would teach, his face would become radiant and clear. . . . Using images and examples in a most skillful manner, he was able to reach out and touch the very hearts of those who would come to hear him teach, thus drawing them into a sense of the richness of the tradition being taught."[7] In 1447, Gedun Drubpa began to build the Tashi Lhunpo Monastery in central Tibet. He worked with the other craftsmen at the monastery, making some of the magnificent statues there. The monastery took many years to complete, and he lived there until his death at the age of eighty-four.

SECOND DALAI LAMA

When Gedun Drubpa died, he had not yet been recognized as the First Dalai Lama. He was simply a leading teacher and spiritual thinker in Tibet. About the time of Gedun Drubpa's death, however, a child named Sangye Pel was born. His father was a holy man. When he was still a boy, Sangye Pel's parents took him to visit a Buddhist temple. There, he told his parents: "You know, I'm not really Sangye Pel. My actual name is Lama Drom."[8] The child believed that he was the reincarnation of Lama Dromtonpa—that is, Lama Dromtonpa had been reborn as this child.

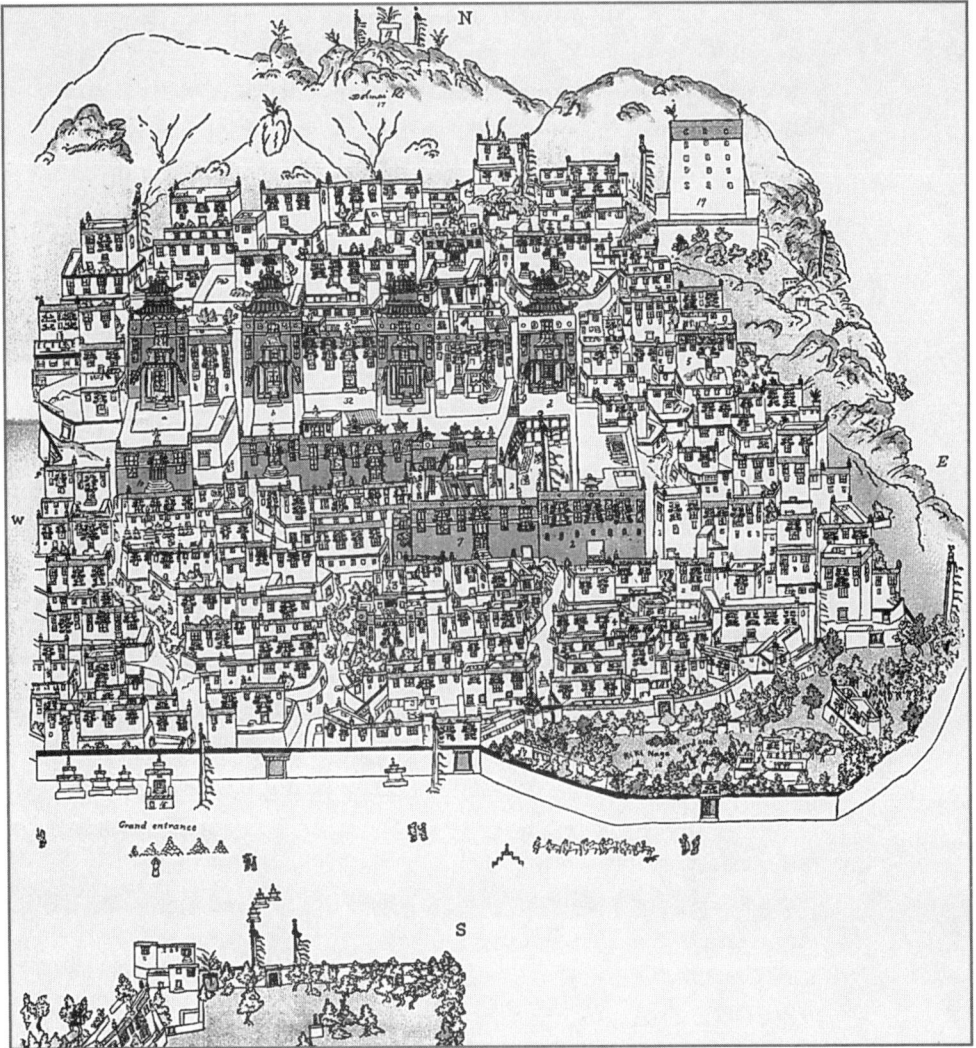

This diagram depicts the outline of the monastery of Tashi Lhunpo, the official seat of the Panchen Lama, the second most important spiritual leader in Tibetan Buddhism. It was founded in 1447 by the First Dalai Lama, Gyalwa Gendun Drup, in Shigatse, Tibet's second largest city. It is one of the four most important monasteries of central Tibet, and was traditionally cared for by the Dalai Lamas and Panchen Lamas of the Gelugpa, or Yellow Hat, School.

Sangye Pel composed songs when he was a small boy that proclaimed the greatness of Buddhist teachings. In addition to claiming to be Lama Dromtonpa reincarnated, the child also said that he was the reincarnation of Gedun Drubpa. Eventually, some of Gedun Drubpa's followers visited Sangye Pel. He knew their names despite the fact that he had never met them before. When the child visited Tashi Lhunpo Monastery, built by the First Dalai Lama, he immediately recognized the Gedun Drubpa's associates, even though it was the first time he had met them. They became convinced that he was indeed the reincarnation of the First Dalai Lama.

Sangye Pel returned to the Tashi Lhunpo Monastery, where he studied and eventually became a monk. He was given a new name, Gedun Gyatso, which means "Sublimely Glorious Ocean." In 1494, he left the monastery and began teaching throughout Tibet. Ten years later, he started to build a great monastery at Gyal. Known as Chokhor Gyal, it sits 15,000 feet (4,575 meters) above sea level in the Himalayas. Nearby was Oracle Lake, where Gedun Gyatso began to have visions. The lake became a place that devout Buddhists have continued to visit, and some say they experience religious visions there. It was at this lake, also known as Lhamo Latso, that visions of the current Dalai Lama were seen by the monks who were searching for him.

When Gedun Gyatso was in his thirties, he became the abbot, or head, of Drepung Loseling Monastery in Lhasa. He died there in 1542.

THIRD DALAI LAMA

About the time that the Second Dalai Lama died, a child was born who succeeded him as the Third Dalai Lama. His name was Ranu Sicho Palzangpo. Even as a young child, the boy already knew some of the important religious beliefs of Tibetan Buddhism. A leading Buddhist lama believed that this boy was the reincarnation of the Second Dalai Lama.

Eventually, the child received a visit from Sunrab Gyatso, who had been the chief minister of the Second Dalai Lama and had helped him build the Gyal Monastery. As Sunrab Gyatso approached, the boy immediately recognized the holy man as well as the other monks who had traveled with him. He also selected a statue that had been a favorite of the Second Dalai Lama from among similar religious objects that did not belong to him.

The boy was taken to Drepung Monastery, where he was proclaimed the new Dalai Lama, Sonam Gyatso, or "Glorious Meritorious Ocean." He then traveled to Gyal Monastery to receive his training. After becoming an ordained monk in his early twenties, Sonam Gyatso began traveling and teaching throughout Tibet. In 1571, Mongol leader Altan Khan invited Sonam Gyatso to visit his headquarters in Mongolia. For centuries, the Mongols had been known for their harsh treatment of other peoples. Once the Mongol Army conquered a city, the Mongols often burned it and murdered its inhabitants. This was a way of instilling fear into the people of other cities so they would surrender to the Mongol armies and not try to fight them.

Sonam Gyatso urged the Mongols to give up their brutal practices and adopt the peaceful ways of Buddhism. During the time he spent in Mongolia, Sonam Gyatso received the title *Dalai Lama* from Altan Khan. This is the Mongol term for "Gyatso." A monastery was established in Mongolia by Altan Khan to honor the Dalai Lama.

The Third Dalai Lama went on to build other religious centers in Tibet. These included the Kumbum Monastery in the eastern part of the country. Later in his life, Sonam Gyatso returned to Mongolia, where he died in 1588.

FOURTH DALAI LAMA

The Fourth Dalai Lama, Yonten Gyatso, was born in Mongolia a year after the death of his predecessor. He was the great-grandson of Altan Khan. As historian Glenn Mullin pointed out, the Tibetans were not pleased that the new Dalai Lama was born in Mongolia, outside their own country.

The Tibetan monk Gushri Palden Gyatso led the team that was sent to decide if this boy was indeed the Dalai Lama. As had been the case in the past, the boy was tested by being shown items that had belonged to the previous Dalai Lama, along with similar ones that did not. In every instance, he selected the correct items. The team believed it had found the Fourth Dalai Lama.[9]

At first, the boy received his training in Mongolia. In 1599, he traveled to Tibet and eventually reached Lhasa. After he arrived, the leading monks appointed a special teacher to continue the boy's education. His name was Lobsang Chokyi Gyaltsen. Later, he was known as the first Panchen Lama. The Panchen Lama became the second most important religious leader in Tibet. Tibetan Buddhists believe that when a Panchen Lama dies, he is reincarnated in his successor, just as the Dalai Lama is. The Panchen Lama and the young Dalai Lama lived together at Deprung Monastery in Lhasa. In 1614, the Dalai Lama became an ordained monk. Only three years later, however, he died.

FIFTH DALAI LAMA

During the lifetime of the Fourth Dalai Lama, Tibet was very unsettled. Rulers who controlled various parts of the country were at war with one another. There were also tensions between the various schools of Tibetan Buddhism. While these conflicts were going on, the Fourth Dalai Lama was reincarnated in a child born in 1617 named Lobzang Gyatso. This boy was taken to the Deprung Monastery, where he received his education under the direction of the Panchen Lama, the same man who had trained the Fourth Dalai Lama.

During the 1620s and 1630s, bloodshed increased in Tibet. One of the rulers called in a group of Mongols to assist him. Then, an unusual event occurred. Instead of attacking Tibet, the Mongol leader, Arsalan Khan, visited the Dalai Lama. He told the Dalai Lama that he wanted to give up his life as a military leader to become a Buddhist monk. Other Mongol commanders followed suit and received the blessings of the Dalai Lama. By 1642, the Mongols had brought the civil war in Tibet to an end.

Following the war, the Dalai Lama was the only leader in Tibet who enjoyed strong support throughout the country. He also had the allegiance of the Mongols. Assisting the Dalai Lama was a monk named Sonam Chopel. He handled many of the Dalai Lama's duties. For example, Sonam Chopel arranged for the Dalai Lama's tours around Tibet and met with many of the rulers of surrounding countries who came to visit the Dalai Lama. Because of his prominent position, Sonam Chopel was called Desi, or "viceroy." In other words, he was the chief minister of the Fifth Dalai Lama.

Sonam Chopel helped the Fifth Dalai Lama become the spiritual and political head of Tibet in the 1640s—the position Dalai Lamas would continue to hold after his tenure. Indeed,

WRITINGS OF THE GREAT FIFTH

The Fifth Dalai Lama wrote far more than any of his predecessors or successors. His writings include works on the Buddhist religion and the importance of meditation as part of Buddhist practices. He also wrote works of history and poetry. The following are lines from one of his poems about Buddhism:

O fortunate ones who take up this supreme way
By means of listening, contemplation and meditation,
Extend your vision beyond the insignificant things
That benefit this one short life alone;
Instill the mind with a sense of firm detachment
And look to the enduring treasures of the spirit. . . .
The root of spiritual fulfillment is simple enough:
Cultivate pure perception of your spiritual teachers;
Cultivate the pure attitude that practices as instructed;
And cultivate the key of making every moment essential.*

* Source: Glenn H. Mullin, *The Fourteen Dalai Lamas*. Santa Fe: Clear Light Publishers, 2001, pp. 224–225.

the Great Fifth, as he is called, was the first to establish the modern role of the Dalai Lama in Tibet. Under his leadership, the first maps of Tibet were drawn. The Fifth Dalai Lama also began a national program of tax collection to provide money for temples, schools, and hospitals.

In 1652, the Great Fifth traveled to China. He visited a special palace—the Yellow Palace—that had been built for him by the Manchu emperor. The emperor told him that the Chinese were going to build many Buddhist temples throughout the empire.

Over the next thirty years, the Great Fifth continued to govern Tibet. He established a new administrative system in Tibet in which the offices of government were run by monks and lay administrators. The Great Fifth also built many new monasteries and temples. When he died in 1682, Tibet was unified and at peace.

POTALA PALACE

Potala Palace sits on a hill outside Lhasa, Tibet. The name of the palace comes from Mount Potala, which, according to Buddhist tradition, is the home of the Bodhisattva Chenresi. The original structure was built by Emperor Songtsen Gampo in 637. In 1645, the Great Fifth began to construct a larger palace that included the original one. The first part of it, known as the White Palace, was finished in 1648. A second structure, called the Red Palace, was built between 1690 and 1694, after the death of the Great Fifth. During the 1920s, the Thirteenth Dalai Lama rebuilt chapels and halls that needed to be repaired. Today, the enormous structure has more than a thousand rooms.

The Red Palace became the home of the Dalai Lamas, who lived on the building's seventh floor. The center of the Tibetan government and a school for the training of Buddhist monks was located in the White Palace.

Potala Palace serves as the final resting place of the bodies of past Dalai Lamas. The palace also houses original copies of the great books that contain the foundational principles of Tibetan Buddhism.

3

Triumph and Turmoil

Love and compassion are necessities, not luxuries.
Without them, humanity cannot survive.
—Tenzin Gyatso, the Fourteenth Dalai Lama

O ver the next decade, the death of the Great Fifth was kept secret. Tibet had been unified only a short time earlier with the Dalai Lama as its religious and political leader. The Great Fifth had feared that as soon as his death was made known, the country might split apart again. Therefore, as he neared the end of his life, the Dalai Lama made his viceroy, Sangye Gyatso, promise not to tell the people of Tibet or any of the nation's powerful neighbors that he had died. After his death, whenever the Dalai Lama was supposed to appear at a public ceremony, a double stood in for him. The rest of the time, the people were told that the Dalai Lama was away on a retreat, praying and meditating.

Meanwhile, Sangye Gyatso continued to do the work of the Great Fifth. This included completing the Potala Palace at Lhasa. At the same time, he also led the search for a new Dalai Lama—but the process was carried out as secretly as possible. An oracle was consulted. (An oracle is a person through whom a deity speaks.) In Tibet, oracles were believed to have the gift of prophecy—that is, they could foretell events. Oracles were often asked to help in the search for a new Dalai Lama. Unfortunately, in this case, the oracle did not provide specific information about who the next Dalai Lama would be. However, he did tell Sangye Gyatso and his associates that the Sixth Dalai Lama would be found in southern Tibet, near the border with the country of Bhutan.

The Sixth Dalai Lama had been born in 1683, a year after the death of the Great Fifth. His father was Lama Tashi Tenzin, a religious leader in the southern part of Tibet. At the age of two, the child was examined by two monks. They concluded that he was not the next Dalai Lama. Though their search continued, they did not find another child who seemed to be the next Dalai Lama. They consulted a holy man who told them that they had already passed over the Sixth Dalai Lama. Eventually, the monks returned to the son of Lama Tashi Tenzin. As they approached and spoke to him, he told them that he was Lobzang Gyatso, the name of the Great Fifth. The boy was carefully examined, then quietly named the Sixth Dalai Lama.

He was trained over the next twelve years, while Tibet was run by Sangye Gyatso. In 1697, Tsangyang Gyatso—"Ocean of Melody"—was finally declared the Sixth Dalai Lama. This may have been a very fitting name for the new Buddhist leader. Throughout Tibet, he soon became known for his melodious poetry. Indeed, his poems are still widely read:

> Words written in black ink
> Are easily destroyed by a small droplet of water;
> But love draws a picture on the heart
> That goes deep and remains forever.[10]

When the time came for the Sixth Dalai Lama to be ordained as a monk, he refused. His associates were stunned. Unlike the earlier Dalai Lamas, the Sixth seemed to be more interested in worldly affairs than spiritual ones. As historian Glenn Mullin wrote: "His passion no longer was the study of Buddhist scriptures; instead during the days he passed his time in archery and horse riding with friends, and at night roamed the streets of Lhasa moving from one tavern to another in search of parties, excitement and beautiful women."[11]

Despite his behavior, the people of Tibet were still convinced that he was the Dalai Lama. Others were not so sure. Lhazang Khan, a powerful leader of the Mongols, was disturbed by the situation in Tibet. As a Buddhist and an important ally of Tibet, Lhazang Khan was rather insulted that he had not been informed when the Great Fifth had died. He also felt that it was disgraceful for the Sixth Dalai Lama to be acting more like a playboy than a devout religious leader.

Lhazang Khan sent messages to the powerful Manchu emperor in China, telling him about the behavior of the Sixth Dalai Lama. With Manchu support, the Khan invaded Tibet during the early 1700s. Sangye Gyatso was captured and beheaded. Lhazang Khan also arrested the Sixth Dalai Lama and removed him from power. Soon afterward, however, a group of Buddhist monks rescued the Dalai Lama and took him to the Deprung Monastery near Lhasa. The monastery was then surrounded by Mongol soldiers, and Lhazang Khan demanded that the Dalai Lama be handed over to him. Rather than risk a battle with the Mongols, the Sixth gave himself up to Lhazang Khan.

As he was taken away by the Mongols, the Sixth Dalai Lama recited a poem:

> *White crane*
> *Lend me your wings*
> *I shall not fly far*
> *From Lithang, I shall return.*[12]

The Sixth Dalai Lama never regained his throne at Potala Palace. After the Mongols took him into captivity, they stopped to make camp. The Dalai Lama began a religious dance, and by the time it had ended, he was dead. However, some Tibetans believe that he actually escaped from the Mongols and went into hiding.

SEVENTH DALAI LAMA

For more than a decade, Lhazang Khan ruled Tibet. In 1706, he installed a new Dalai Lama—Yeshe Gyatso—to replace the leader he had removed from Lhasa. Although Lhazang Khan

IPPOLITO DESIDERI

In 1716, a Catholic missionary named Ippolito Desideri came to Lhasa to spread the Christian religion to Tibet. The Portuguese monk had traveled from Rome to India before arriving in Tibet. After meeting the monk, Lhazang Khan allowed him to set up a Catholic mission in Lhasa. Desideri learned the Tibetan language. He also received permission from the Khan to participate in a debate with Buddhist monks about the values of Catholicism as opposed to Buddhism. Desideri had to spend many months training in the techniques of debate. Buddhist monks became skilled debaters as part of their regular education. Despite his hard work, the debate was never held because civil war broke out in Tibet. After five years of living inside the country, Desideri was forced to flee. He never returned.

considered Yeshe Gyatso the Seventh Dalai Lama, the people of Tibet never recognized him as a legitimate leader.

Tibetans resented the rule of Lhazang Khan. To try to save Tibet, Buddhist monks called on another Mongolian leader, Tsewang Rabten, to bring an army into Tibet and remove Lhazang Khan. In 1717, Lhazang Khan's army was defeated and Lhazang Khan himself was executed. However, the victors remained in Lhasa, where they killed hundreds of innocent civilians.

Lhazung Khan's appointed Dalai Lama, however, was removed. A new Dalai Lama had been found in Lithang, in eastern Tibet. The boy had been born in 1708, two years after the death of the Sixth Dalai Lama. The child's grandfather had been a friend of the Great Fifth. The new spiritual leader was taken to Kumbum Monastery, near the Chinese border, for religious training.

Three years later, the Manchu emperor of China sent an army into Tibet. The Mongols were defeated, and at that time, Lobsang Kalsang Gyatso officially became the Seventh Dalai Lama of Tibet.

The Manchus helped establish a new government in the country. While the Dalai Lama was in overall charge of Tibet, a council of ministers handled the day-to-day tasks of governing the nation. Two years later, the Manchus took their troops out of Tibet, leaving only two Chinese *ambans*—ambassadors—in Lhasa to represent Manchu interests.

Over the next twenty years, the council of ministers was controlled by a very powerful leader named Phola. As authors Roger Hicks and Ngakpa Chogyam explained, he "was far too ready to rely on the Chinese for advice, and the Seventh was not particularly interested in worldly affairs. As a result, Chinese influence steadily grew; and when it looked as if the Seventh might take a hand in the government of the country, [Phola] persuaded him to make several extended journeys which kept him safely out of Lhasa for years at a time." [13]

Lobsang Kalsang Gyatso is considered one of the greatest teachers among the Dalai Lamas. He would speak to large crowds of Tibetans and travel around the country providing spiritual direction for his people. Frequently, he did not dress in the finery appropriate for the Dalai Lama, but instead walked among Tibetans pretending to be a simple monk or homeless beggar. People sometimes invited him to stay with them and fed him in their homes.

In 1747, Phola died and was succeeded by his son. However, the Chinese ambans did not like the new chief minister and murdered him three years later. At that time, a mass demonstration occurred in Lhasa. The demonstrators seized the ambans and killed them. As a result, the Dalai Lama took control of the government back from the Manchus. He continued to direct political affairs until he died in 1757.

EIGHTH DALAI LAMA

Following the death of the Seventh Dalai Lama, a regent—a temporary substitute ruler—was selected by the political and religious leaders of the country to run Tibet. His name was Demo Tulku Delek Gyatso. Even as he took on his new responsibilities, he began the traditional effort to find the next Dalai Lama.

The child who would become the Eighth Dalai Lama was born in 1758, a year after the death of the Seventh. The boy was examined by the Panchen Lama and declared the eighth spiritual leader of Tibet. He was then taken to Potala Palace. Over the next three decades, while the Dalai Lama was receiving his spiritual training, regents directed the government of Tibet.

During the 1780s, Tibet faced an invasion from the Gurkhas who ruled Nepal. (Gurkhas were native Nepalese soldiers who served in the British or Indian army.) In response, the Dalai Lama asked the Manchu government in China for temporary military aid. In 1792, the Chinese stepped into the conflict. They sent a large army that drove the Gurkhas back to Nepal.

In return for rescuing Tibet, the Manchu emperor began to assume a symbolic role in the selection of the Dalai Lama. He sent a golden bowl to Tibet. If there were several candidates for the position of Dalai Lama, their names were to be placed in the bowl. Then one name would be drawn by the selection team and the new spiritual leader chosen.

During the Eighth Dalai Lama's years of leadership, he built Norbu Lingka ("Jewel Palace"). This was the summer palace, which served as a center for much of his teaching. Future Dalai Lamas spent the winter months at Potala and the summer months at Norbu Lingka.

DALAI LAMAS NINE THROUGH TWELVE

The Eighth Dalai Lama died in 1804. About a year later, the Ninth Dalai Lama was born in southern Tibet. As a child, he was taken to Lhasa to begin his religious training. When he was just nine years old, he caught pneumonia and died. A regent had been governing Tibet while the Dalai Lama was in training. Now the regent had to begin another search for a new Dalai Lama.

Together with the Panchen Lama, the regent consulted the oracles, who agreed that the new religious leader would be found in the eastern part of the country. In fact, the Tenth Dalai Lama had been born near Litang Monastery. The search team discovered three boys, each of whom had the potential to be the Dalai Lama. Finally, they settled on Gyalwa Tsultrim Gyatso. He turned out to be sickly and died in 1837 at the age of sixteen.

Once again, the Tibetan regent had to search for another Dalai Lama. The Eleventh was eventually discovered and put into training like his predecessors. In 1855, he finally took over as the political and religious leader of Tibet. Unfortunately, in 1856, he, too, died before reaching adulthood.

Another search began, this time in the area south of Lhasa. White clouds had appeared over the city, spelling out *Ol*, which was viewed as a sign that the new Dalai Lama had been born in Olkha in southern Tibet. A search team of monks found a boy there whom they believed was the incarnation of the Dalai

Lama. Like the Dalai Lama candidates before him, he was tested by being shown items that had belonged to his predecessor, along with similar objects that had not belonged to the Eleventh Dalai Lama. Each time, the boy selected the correct item. The boy was then taken to Lhasa so he could be trained to serve as the Twelfth Dalai Lama.

Meanwhile, political problems were taking a toll on the country. At this time, Tibet was being ruled by a regent and a cabinet of ministers. One of the cabinet officials, Wangchuk Gyalpo Shetra, tried to remove the regent, who had grown very powerful. At first, the regent fought off this attempt. Shetra, however, gathered an army, marched on Lhasa, and forcibly ousted the regent from power.

Shetra then ruled as regent until his death in 1864, after which other powerful ministers took his place. In 1873, the Twelfth Dalai Lama finally took personal control as Tibet's leader. Less than three years later, before he could bring political stability to the country, he died.

Historians have speculated as to why four Dalai Lamas in fairly rapid succession died before any of them could reach adulthood. One theory holds that they were poisoned by agents of the Manchu emperor in order to keep Tibet weak. According to another theory, they might have been murdered by the regents, who wanted to retain power for themselves. A third theory is that Tibet was being exposed at the time to increasingly large numbers of travelers from other countries, who were bringing with them new diseases. Most Tibetans had not been exposed to these diseases, and as a result, their immune systems had not built up a tolerance for them. These new illnesses may have killed the Dalai Lamas.

During the nineteenth century, Tibet became a prize in the so-called "Great Game" between Russia and Great Britain. This was a rivalry between the two greatest imperialistic powers of the time for control of central Asia. The British had conquered India and wanted to protect their colony's northern border by sending traders into Tibet and developing an alliance with the country. To the north of Tibet, Russia had taken over the lands that had previously been controlled by the Mongols. Russia now wanted to protect its southern border. As the center of the Buddhist faith that was practiced by the Mongol tribes, Tibet was valuable to the Russians in that it might help keep the Mongols under control.

BRITAIN, RUSSIA, AND THE THIRTEENTH DALAI LAMA

In 1876, the Thirteenth Dalai Lama was born southeast of Lhasa. To find the boy, the traditional search committee traveled to Oracle Lake. There, members of the search team saw visions in the water that were shaped like the villages and mountains around the child's birthplace. The boy was eventually discovered and tested in the traditional method by being shown the possessions of his predecessor. In 1877, the boy and his family were taken to Lhasa and he was given the name Thupten Gyatso. It means "Fearless and Powerful One, Glorious Guru Victorious in All Ways." He would prove himself worthy of the name, becoming one of the most memorable Dalai Lamas in the history of Tibet. For this reason, he is called the Great Thirteenth.

While the new Dalai Lama was receiving his religious training, the political situation in Tibet continued to grow more unstable. In 1876, the British had signed an agreement with China called the Chefoo Convention. Great Britain realized that it had little direct influence in Tibet. Therefore, as part of the Chefoo Convention, the British agreed to recognize China's power there, regarding Tibet as part of the Chinese Empire. The Tibetans violently disagreed. They considered their country independent. The British, however, were convinced that the Chefoo Convention would allow them to rely on the Chinese to keep the Russians out of Tibet. As part of the agreement, the British received permission from the Chinese to begin exploring Tibet.

Meanwhile, both the British and the Russians tried to increase their influence in Tibet. During the 1880s, the British wanted to establish a trading post in Tibet and expected the Chinese to help them by putting pressure on the Tibetans. The Tibetan government refused to be pressured, though.

In the 1890s, Russian influence in Tibet began to increase. One of the Dalai Lama's teachers was a Mongolian monk named Ghomang Lobzang. Although he went by several names, the Russians called him Dorjieff. He led a Tibetan diplomatic party to Russia, where the representatives met with Tsar Nicholas II in September 1900. The British feared that Tibet was about to sign a treaty with Russia. Indeed, the Tibetans believed that the Russian tsar might offer their country protection from other nations.

In 1903, a British force led by Major Francis Younghusband was sent north from India to Tibet. Younghusband's mission was to sign a trade agreement with the Dalai Lama and prevent the Russians from gaining any influence over the spiritual leader. Meanwhile, the Dalai Lama had left Tibet and gone to Mongolia. As a result, when Younghusband arrived, there was no one in authority to sign an agreement with the British. Nor were the Chinese able to convince the Tibetan government to agree to a trade mission. Therefore, early in 1904, Younghusband and his troops advanced northward toward Lhasa.

Their march was barred by a Tibetan army, and a battle broke out in which about three hundred Tibetan soldiers were killed. The Tibetans retreated but struck the British once more as they marched northward. Once again, the Tibetans were defeated. Eventually, Younghusband managed to reach Lhasa. In 1904, he was successful in signing a trade agreement with the regent of Tibet, who had taken temporary control of Tibet after the Thirteenth Dalai Lama fled upon hearing news of Younghusband's approach. The British were given permission to set up trading stations in several Tibetan towns. After the agreement was signed, the British went back to India.

After the Dalai Lama went to Mongolia, he continued to travel for the next five years. He taught and blessed devout Buddhists throughout Tibet. The Chinese invited him to their capital at Peking (present-day Beijing), which he visited in 1908. A short time later, Tibet was invaded by a Chinese warlord who took control of Lhasa in 1910. This time, the Dalai Lama fled south to India and lived at Darjeeling for the next four years. He called on the British to stop the Chinese and help save his country, but Great Britain did nothing.

MAJOR YOUNGHUSBAND

Francis Younghusband was born in 1863 in northwestern India and became an officer in the British Army at the age of nineteen. Much of his time was spent exploring parts of central Asia, surveying and mapping the land, while gathering information about Chinese and Russian military power in these areas. The British needed this data to help them protect their empire in India.

During 1886, Younghusband traveled across Manchuria and visited the Chinese capital of Peking (present-day Beijing). The following year, he explored western China, traveling through the Gobi Desert and into high mountainous regions that no European had visited before. Soon afterward, he became a member of England's prestigious Royal Geographical Society. This group included some of the world's greatest explorers.

In 1889, Younghusband led a small military force northward to stop a group of bandits who were attacking local merchants trading with the British. He was also expected to determine whether Russian secret agents were operating in the area. There, he met one of the top Russian agents, a Captain Gromchevsky. "As I rode up," Younghusband wrote, "a tall, fine-looking bearded man in Russian uniform came out to meet me." The two men ate dinner together. It "was a very substantial meal," Younghusband wrote.*

Later, Younghusband entered the country of Hunza, north of India. Its ruler, Safdar Ali, was sending bandits against the merchants as well as dealing with the Russians. Younghusband ordered Safdar Ali to call off his bandits or they would be attacked by British troops. Then he returned to India.

Because of his experience, Younghusband was chosen in 1904 to command the British expedition to Tibet. Later, he would make three unsuccessful attempts to climb Mount Everest in Nepal, the world's highest mountain.

* Source: Peter Hopkirk, *The Great Game: The Struggle for Empire in Central Asia.* New York: Kodansha International, 1994, p. 455.

Meanwhile, the political situation in China was changing. In 1911, the Chinese emperor was overthrown and a new government took power. Chinese troops in Tibet no longer supported the occupation of the country. Tibetan troops also rose up and overran the Chinese military outposts. The Tibetan uprising was encouraged by the Dalai Lama from his residence in India.

Finally, in 1912, the Dalai Lama returned to Tibet. He soon formally declared the nation's independence. As part of this proclamation, he called on Tibet to improve its military forces to protect the country.

The Great Thirteenth also began other reforms. For example, he appointed inspectors in the government to keep an eye on the civil servants and make sure they were serving the Tibetan people honestly and fairly.

For the next twenty years, the Thirteenth Dalai Lama ruled Tibet. It remained independent, and the Chinese were prevented from entering the country. Tibet operated as a theocracy—the Dalai Lama directed both the religious and political life of the nation.

4

Buddhism

This is my simple religion.
There is no need for temples;
no need for complicated philosophy.
Our own brain, our own heart is our temple;
the philosophy is kindness.

—Tenzin Gyatso, the Fourteenth Dalai Lama

For centuries, the Dalai Lama has been one of the principal leaders of Buddhism. According to historians, the Buddha—Siddhartha Gautama—lived during the fifth and sixth centuries B.C. and died around 483 B.C. Siddhartha was born in Nepal, a mountainous country south of Tibet that borders India. He was the son of a local king, who brought him up in great luxury. In fact, Siddhartha's father tried to prevent him from learning about the suffering that people may experience in life. He never saw poverty, old age, or death. Under this protective veil, Siddhartha married, had a child, and prepared himself to eventually take over his father's kingdom.

When he was still a young man, however, Siddhartha ventured outside his father's palace, and beyond the castle walls, he saw an old man. Then he saw another man who was suffering from disease. Finally, he happened upon the body of a person who had died. These experiences greatly troubled Siddhartha until he met a beggar who had given up all of his worldly desires and achieved inner peace.

Siddhartha decided that this was the path he must take in his own life. He decided to move out of the palace, leaving behind his riches and his family, to seek salvation in a life of poverty. For the next six years, he ate and drank very little and almost died of starvation. Realizing that this ascetic approach had brought him no closer to enlightenment, Siddhartha began to eat and drink again. Eventually, he adopted a middle ground between eating almost nothing and indulging in too much luxury.

One day, Siddhartha sat down under the branches of a tree and began to meditate on the meaning of life and the way to enlightenment. There, he battled the forces of Mara, a supernatural being who tried to tempt him. Siddhartha was finally able to defeat Mara's attempts to corrupt him, and as a result, he achieved enlightenment. From that time on, he became known as the Buddha, which means "Awakened One" or "Enlightened One."

TEACHINGS OF THE BUDDHA

The Buddha soon began to gather followers whom he instructed in his beliefs. One of the main principles is known as *dharma.*

This refers to a person's duty or proper condition within the universe. The early teachings of the Buddha are called the "First Turning of the Dharma Wheel." The Buddha believed that existence is like a wheel. Human beings are continuously being born, suffering, growing old, dying, and being reborn into more suffering. He called this human condition *samsara*. Buddhists believe that people can be reborn into various types of existence. These may include human beings who live on Earth or gods who live in heaven. In addition, individuals may be reborn as demons, who are controlled by their anger and have very unhappy lives. They might also be reborn as restless spirits who roam the earth or live in hell—or even as animals.

The form in which an individual is reborn depends on *karma*. This means "action." There are good actions, or good karma, and bad actions, or bad karma. By *action*, Buddhists refer not only to what an individual does, but also to what he or she thinks or says. Every action has a consequence. By performing good actions, people can build up credit. The more good karma they produce, the more likely it is they will be reborn as a human being or as a god. The more bad karma, the better the chance that they will be reborn as a spirit suffering in hell. As the Fourteenth Dalai Lama himself has written: "The ultimate purpose, or aim, of existence is to achieve a favorable birth in our next life, a goal that can only be attained by restraining from actions that are harmful to others." [14]

Eventually, human beings with enough good karma can break the cycle of samsara and reach *nirvana*—the state of perfect enlightenment. Individuals who have achieved nirvana are no longer reborn over and over again. Once nirvana is achieved, the individual personality disappears, bringing the person into an ultimate state of perfect bliss.

THE FOUR NOBLE TRUTHS

The foundation of Buddhism is the Four Noble Truths that were originally taught by the Buddha. According to the First Noble Truth, all life involves suffering. This concept is known as *duhkha*. As author Todd Lewis puts it, "Humanity is trapped in the potentially endless cycle of *samsara* and must endure lifetime after lifetime of suffering and unsatisfactoriness . . . in all their forms. [This] alerts the Buddhist to the inevitable experience of mortal existence: physical and mental disease, loss of loved ones, bodily degeneration in old age, and inescapable death." [15]

The Second Noble Truth states that all the suffering in the world is caused by human desires. These primarily include a desire for material possessions, money, power, fame, and bodily pleasure. Although acquiring these things may provide temporary satisfaction, that feeling quickly passes away. As a result, the individual is only left unhappy and wanting more. Among the most harmful human desires are lust, hatred, jealousy, and enmity toward other people. If desire can be eliminated, Buddhists believe that individuals can achieve nirvana.

The Third Noble Truth assures the faithful that desires can, in fact, be overcome. Nirvana describes a state of ultimate peace and freeing oneself from desire and suffering. The word *nirvana* actually means "to cool," which refers to cooling human desires, eliminating bad karma, and escaping from samsara. [16]

According to the Fourth Noble Truth, the way to eliminate desire and ultimately to reach nirvana is to follow the "Noble Eightfold Path."

THE NOBLE EIGHTFOLD PATH

According to Buddhist beliefs, every individual can follow a path that will lead to nirvana. It includes eight ideals that are divided into three parts.

The first part is morality. It consists of three aspects: right speech, right action (or conduct), and right livelihood. By *right speech*, Buddhists mean speaking only kind words to other people and not gossiping about them. *Right action* means that people should do nothing that harms others. As the Fourteenth Dalai Lama explains, the Buddha had two sayings: "If possible, you should help others. If that is not possible, at least you should do no harm." [17] Among the requirements needed to fulfill right action are the Five Precepts: not to destroy life, not to steal, not to lie, not to drink or use drugs, and not to engage in improper sexual activity.

The second section of the "Noble Eightfold Path" involves meditation, which has three components. These include right effort, right mindfulness, and right concentration. Meditation is one of the most important elements of Buddhism. A Buddhist meditates by sitting cross-legged and tuning out the distractions of everyday life. Using a chant or a *mantra*—a syllable or word repeated over and over—Buddhists concentrate on life's deeper meaning. Meditation enables Buddhists to achieve a sense of calm and peacefulness, which they believe leads to insight or wisdom.

Insight is based on understanding what the Buddha called "three marks of existence." These were suffering, impermanence, and the nonself. By *impermanence*, the Buddha meant that all life is constantly changing. Individuals, for example, pass from one existence to another. Therefore, it is pointless to become attached to any one object. When they speak of the *nonself*, Buddhists mean that a person should have no identity that is separate from others. Individual identity leads only to selfishness, too much attention to oneself, and a lack of concern for other people. Once individuals free themselves of self-centeredness, they can open up to other human beings. This leads to compassion and empathy, which are at the center of the Buddhist way of life. These emotions enable Buddhists to produce good karma. As the current Dalai Lama wrote:

> The self-cherishing attitude obstructs us from generating genuine empathy towards others and limits our outlook to the narrow confines of our own self-centered concerns. In essence, . . . we seek to transform our normal selfish outlook on life into a more altruistic one, which, at the very least, regards the welfare of others as equal in importance to our own, and ideally regards others' welfare as much more important than ours. [18]

By fulfilling this aim, we can eventually reach the last part of the "Noble Eightfold Path"—wisdom. This includes right views and right thought (or aspirations). Individuals who possess wisdom can achieve nirvana. When they follow the path of wisdom, everyone understands that the three marks of existence can never be changed. Individuals also recognize their interconnectedness to all other human beings and their universal responsibility to help others.

TIBETAN BUDDHISM

Most Buddhists live in Asia. One school of Buddhism is called *Theravada*, meaning "Way of the Elders." It spread throughout Southeast Asia into Thailand, Vietnam, Cambodia, and Sri Lanka. Another school of Buddhism is *Mahayana*, or "The Great Vehicle." It has believers in Tibet, Mongolia, China, and Japan. Buddhists do not believe in a single, all-powerful god, as some religions do. Unlike Christianity, there is no belief in a god who created everything. Instead, adherents of the faith believe in Buddhas (those who have achieved nirvana—they are not gods) and certain deities (none of which is a supreme god).

Tibetan Buddhists also believe in *bodhisattvas*. These are individuals who have reached enlightenment and have the ability to achieve nirvana. However, out of compassion for other people, they have chosen to be reincarnated as teachers or religious leaders so they can help others achieve nirvana. In Tibet, these teachers are called *tulkus*. The Dalai Lama, for example, is believed to be the reincarnation of the bodhisattva Avalokiteshvara, the deity of compassion. Each Dalai Lama is also considered the reincarnation of his predecessors. As author John Peacock has written: "The first step on the path of the *bodhisattva* is the development of *bodhichitta* or 'awakening mind.' What the development of *bodhichitta* marks is a fundamental shift in focus from self-concern to concern for the suffering of others, which manifests itself as compassion." [19]

BUDDHIST WORSHIP

Some Buddhists become monks and nuns. They live in monasteries, called *sanghas*. The Dalai Lamas all receive their training in these sanghas before assuming spiritual and political leadership in Tibet.

Children may enter a monastery at the age of seven or eight. At one time, approximately 20 percent of men in Tibet became monks.

Buddhist monks and nuns have their heads shaved and vow to live a life of celibacy. They agree to fast after their meal at midday and not to accept money or wear perfume or jewelry. They also sleep very little and usually on mats or pads that offer little comfort. Monks are permitted to own only eight items: three robes, a belt, a razor, a filter to strain living organisms from their water, a sewing kit made up of just a needle and thread, and an alms bowl in which to collect food. The monks spend part of the day maintaining the monastery, but during much of the rest of the time they meditate and teach others.

Monks study the *Tripitaka* (called the *Tipitaka* in the Theravada School of Buddhism). These are the earliest known Buddhist teachings and they outline the rules that monks are expected to live by; the ideas of the Buddha, or *sutras* (teachings); and analyses of these words by learned teachers.

The Tripitaka is a set of texts that provide the basic doctrines of Buddhist thought. There are three divisions within the Tripitaka, which are often referred to as the "Three Baskets" (*Tripitaka*, in fact, means "three baskets"). The first is the *Vinaya Pitaka*, which contains rules that are used to govern everyday life for Buddhist monks and nuns. These rules are intended to establish a harmonious monastic community. The second part of the Tripitaka is the *Sutta Pitaka*. This is a collection of verses attributed to the Buddha and his earliest and closest followers. Made up of more than ten thousand individual verses, the *Sutta Pitaka* covers topics that range from biographical details of the Buddha's life to techniques for appropriate meditative breathing. The final division of the Tripitaka is the *Abhidhamma Pitaka*. This set of teachings is closely related to the *Sutta Pitaka*. In fact, the *Abhidhamma Pitaka* essentially contains reorganized and more detailed versions of the verses found in the *Sutta Pitaka*. Its aim is to provide the faithful with a coherent system for following the teachings laid out in the *Vinaya Pitaka* and *Sutta Pitaka*.

One of the most important writings for Tibetan Buddhists is the *Lotus Sutra*. It contains many parables that present and explain the teachings of Buddhism. The lotus is one of the symbols of Buddhism. It is a beautiful flower that grows and blossoms in the mud. The life cycle of this plant serves as a metaphor for achieving nirvana through the sufferings of human existence. In fact, the Dalai Lama is known as the "holder of the white lotus."

Buddhist symbols help followers define their faith. One important Buddhist symbol in Tibet is the *mandala*. This is a large diagram that depicts the Wheel of the Law—a wheel with eight spokes representing the Noble Eightfold Path as well as the different divine powers that are at work in the universe. The mandala depicts the totality of existence, both inner and outer.

Buddhists gather together to worship and meditate at a temple. One of the most famous is Jokhang Temple, located in Lhasa. At 1,300 years old, it is Tibet's most ancient and holiest shrine. Each day, Tibetan Buddhists approach the temple and prostrate themselves before it. This is the first step in the traditional daily worship ritual. Then, worshipers walk around the outside of the temple in a clockwise direction, while spinning a prayer wheel. The wheel contains prayers written on a paper scroll. Buddhists may also carry rosary beads, which they finger during meditation. Outside, the temple is decorated with flags that contain Buddhist prayers. Inside are shrines with statues of the Buddha, called *Buddharupas*. Tibetan temples also contain large prayer wheels and candles made of butter. Worshipers remove their shoes as they enter a temple, then sit on the floor. Butter candles are lighted during the Buddhist ceremonies, bells are rung, and flowers are placed at the foot of the Buddharupas. Monks direct the religious ceremonies, read excerpts from the sacred writings, and lead the meditation for the worshipers, who chant and recite their mantras.

In addition to group worship, Tibetan Buddhists often maintain shrines in their homes. These include a Buddharupa.

Although few Buddhists still practice daily worship, traditionally it included a presentation of flowers as an offering, the ritual burning of incense, and readings from sacred writings.

However, worship alone is not enough to produce good karma. Buddhists are also expected to perform good acts. They must support monks and lamas with alms—that is, donations of food. As part of their religious beliefs, Buddhists make pilgrimages, or journeys, to sacred temples and monasteries. Here, devout Buddhists prostrate themselves—lying flat on the

TANTRAS

Some Tibetan Buddhists take a special approach to worship, called Tantric Buddhism. This practice is based on a group of writings called the *tantras*. These are thought to be the secret teachings of the Buddha. Although the full texts are available only to the initiated, there are thousands of tantric works that discuss mystical topics such as "sky dogs" and "cosmic tortoises."*

Tantric Buddhism began in India during the seventh century and gradually moved into Tibet over the next two hundred years. According to author Todd Lewis, "Tantric Buddhists aim to attain enlightenment rapidly in a single lifetime through powerful techniques learned under the guidance of an accomplished . . . saint [teacher]."** Worshipers often must memorize one of the tantras in order to gain admission into this special Buddhist school. The tantric school is often called *Vajrayana*, which means "Diamond-Thunderbolt Vehicle." The diamond is a precious jewel that is harder than any other. It cannot be destroyed; in fact, it has the power to break any other gem.

A large portion of the tantras deal with special methods of meditation. Buddhists learn how to create an image in their mind of a tantric god, then imagine that they *are* that god in order to demonstrate the characteristics associated with him. One of the deities often used is the god Mahakala, or "Great Time." He safeguards the Buddhist temples and monasteries and is considered one of the most important deities in Tibet.

* Source: Edward Conze, "Buddhism: The Mahāyāna," *Encyclopedia of the World's Religions*, ed. R.C. Zaehner. New York: Barnes & Noble Books, 1997, p. 296.

** Kevin Trainor, ed., *Buddhism: The Illustrated Guide*. New York: Oxford University Press, 2001, p. 162.

ground with their heads down—as they pray to the Buddha. The faithful also visit *stupas*—shrines that contain ancient relics from the Buddha, or Buddhist writings. Visiting these sites is part of an effort by devout Buddhists to follow the Eightfold Noble Path, which calls for right actions.

Buddhists also participate in festivals each year. In Tibet, these

LOSAR AT POTALA PALACE

When the Fourteenth Dalai Lama arrived at Potala Palace, he was accompanied by his mother, father, and brothers. The Dalai Lama's mother described the family's first celebration of Losar at the palace:

> The ceremony opened with prostrations to His Holiness by all those gathered, in order of rank—government staff, [foreign officials,] and Muslim and Chinese representatives. Everyone presented His Holiness with a scarf [a traditional gift], and he gave blessings, all of which could take two to three hours. During the ceremony we were served all sorts of delicacies at regular intervals. . . . After the drummers and dancers had performed, . . . [w]e then returned home, because this first day of Losar was when we had to receive callers—aristocratic families and government officials. . . . On the second day of Losar we all attended a ceremony at the Potala at eight in the morning. . . . *Domadesi* [pastry] and Tibetan tea were served as well as other delicacies, such as fried bread filled with meat. On this day the state oracles made predictions for the coming year. We again received callers, as on the first day, and members of the family took New Year offerings to the Kashag [Tibetan cabinet] and government officials as well as to the lamas. On the fourth day of New Year began Monlam, the Great Prayer Festival. Strict rules had to be observed by everyone during Monlam: no noise, including no barking dogs and no singing, and no intoxicating spirits. The night before, monks came from other monasteries to Lhasa, where they were housed with local families. Early the next morning the lamas proceeded to the Jokhang, and soon all three of its floors were teeming with monks, like ants on a hill.*

* Source: Diki Tsering, *Dalai Lama, My Son,* New York: Penguin, 2000, pp. 119–121.

include Losar, the New Year celebration that occurs at the full moon in February. Losar is viewed as a time for people to cleanse themselves of any bad deeds committed during the previous year and to welcome the New Year. Just before the actual festival begins, the people take a day for quiet reflection while monks chant and dance to ritually drive away negativity. The fifteen-day event that follows includes dancing, plays about the life of the Buddha, puppet shows and magnificent parades, as well as horseracing and footraces. People do a thorough cleaning of their houses, too.

Although Losar is generally considered Tibetan Buddhism's most important holiday, there are many other celebrations in Tibet—most of them lively, colorful events. Four of the best-known holidays are commemorations of the four so-called "great deeds" of the Buddha. According to legend, the Buddha performed a miracle on each of these four days to inspire stronger faith among his followers. Among this set of holidays is Chotrul Duchen ("great occasion"), which marks the fifteenth day of the Tibetan New Year.

One other major Tibetan festival is Wesak, which traditionally takes place at the full moon in May, although it sometimes is held in April. This day celebrates the triple anniversary of the Buddha's birth, enlightenment, and death.

THE DALAI LAMA AND TIBETAN BUDDHISM

Over the centuries, there have been various groups, or schools, of Buddhist monks inside Tibet. In earlier times, the Sakyapa group was the most powerful. The Gelugpa group became the most important during the life of the Great Fifth. This group was led by the Dalai Lama, who went on to become the most important religious leader for all Buddhists in Tibet. The Buddhist monks also exercised political power in the country. As author Todd Lewis put it, this was "the only time in the Buddhist world when the Sangha [religious community] assumed secular power."[20] However, the Dalai Lamas also realized that the political independence could not be maintained unless Tibet built a strong army. The Great Thirteenth tried to develop this army to defend the country against possible invasion. As he wrote just before his death:

> It may happen that here in Tibet, religion and government will be attacked both from without and within. Unless we guard our own country, it will now happen that the Dalai and Panchen Lamas, the Father and Son, and all revered holders of the Faith, will disappear and become nameless. . . . All beings will be sunk in great hardship and overwhelming fear; the days and nights will drag on slowly in suffering.[21]

Unfortunately, his fears would be realized when he was succeeded by the Fourteenth Dalai Lama.

5

Tenzin Gyatso

For as long as space endures
And for as long as living beings remain,
Until then may I too abide
To dispel the misery of the world.

—A Tibetan Buddhist prayer

Tenzin Gyatso began living in Potala Palace when he was just a child. As he recalled years later,

> I was given the Great Fifth's own bedroom on the seventh (top) story. It was pitifully cold and ill-lit and I doubt whether it can have been touched since his time. Everything in it was ancient and decrepit and, behind the drapes that hung across each of the four walls lay deposits of centuries-old dust. At one end of the room stood an altar. On it were set small butter lamps (bowls of rancid . . . butter into which a wick was set and lighted) and little dishes of food and water placed in offering to the Buddhas. Every day these would be plundered by mice. I became very fond of these little creatures. They were beautiful and showed no fear as they helped themselves to their daily rations.[22]

After entering the palace, Tenzin Gyatso became a novice monk. This involved a "taking of refuge," or dedication to the Three Jewels of Buddhism. These are the Buddha; the dharma; and the sangha, or religious community. Tenzin Gyatso was also assigned two tutors to direct his education. One of them became regent of Tibet while the Dalai Lama was still a child. This tutor was replaced by Ling Rinpoché, a stern taskmaster. "I was really scared of him," the Dalai Lama later admitted. "I became afraid even at the sight of his servant and quickly learned to recognize the sound of his footsteps—at which my heart missed a beat."[23]

The Dalai Lama's tutors educated him according to a traditional curriculum that included five major subjects: Tibetan art and culture; Sanskrit, the ancient Indian language of the Buddhist teachings; medicine; logic; and Buddhist philosophy. There were also five minor subjects: music, poetry, dialectics (the skill of debating), theater, and astrology—the study of how the stars influence events on Earth. In the morning, the child practiced penmanship, reading, and writing. Then he would be required to memorize a section of Buddhist scripture. Later in the morning, Tenzin Gyatso would recite the lines he had memorized earlier to one of his tutors. During the afternoon, a tutor would instruct the Dalai Lama in the skills of debating and public speaking by preparing him to discuss an important topic in religion or philosophy.

By his own admission, Tenzin Gyatso was not an outstanding student; he did only enough to pass. To motivate him to work harder, one of his tutors "organized a mock exam in which I was to compete with [one of the household servants]. Unknown to me, [my tutor] had briefed him fully beforehand, with the result that I lost the contest. I was devastated, especially as my humiliation was public. The trick succeeded and for a time I worked very hard out of sheer anger."[24] Eventually, however, he went back to his old ways.

The Dalai Lama spent part of each year at the Tibetan Summer Palace, Norbu Lingka, which he liked much better than Potala. The Summer Palace had beautiful ponds as well as parks filled with peacocks, Mongolian camels, and other animals. Sometimes he would fish from the banks of a pond or take a small boat out on the water. As a teenager, he once went into the garage without permission, and began driving one of the cars around the grounds of the palace. Unfortunately, he crashed into a tree and smashed a headlight. Luckily for him, he was able to find a piece of glass and repair the light so that no one ever found out what had happened.

To protect him from danger and to ensure that he was educated properly, Tenzin Gyatso was never allowed to leave the palace and interact with the ordinary people of Tibet; at least not until he had grown older. To fulfill his curiosity about the outside world, the best he could do was watch the residents of Lhasa through a telescope from Potala Palace.

In his autobiography, the Dalai Lama recalled the many holidays that were part of the Tibetan calendar. The length of each month was based on the moon's phases. Each year was named after one of five elements—earth, air, fire, water, and iron. Years were also named after one of twelve animals—

mouse, ox, tiger, hare, dragon, serpent, horse, sheep, monkey, bird, dog, and pig. With the combination of element and animal, a year might be called, for example, Iron Dragon. Every year there was the New Year celebration known as Losar, and Monlam—the Great Prayer Festival. There was also an opera festival at which dancers and singers performed. It lasted for an entire week. High Tibetan government officials and their wives would dress in their finest clothes during the opera festival to show off their wealth and impress one another.

During the time that the Dalai Lama sat on the Lion Throne, Tibet was made up of various classes of people. The population of the monasteries included monks and nuns, as well as abbots,

HEINRICH HARRER AND THE DALAI LAMA

In 1944, an Austrian mountain climber named Heinrich Harrer began traveling in Tibet. Two years later, he arrived at Lhasa. He was one of the few people from the West to reach the so-called "forbidden city." Most people needed a special pass from the Tibetan government to come to Lhasa. When he arrived, he was fortunate to meet an important government official who welcomed Harrer warmly and invited the explorer to stay with him. Eventually, the Dalai Lama's parents heard of Harrer's presence in the city and invited him to their home. He began a friendly relationship with the young Dalai Lama.

In 1948, Harrer was called to the Summer Palace, which suffered from flooding during the rainy season in Tibet. With the help of Tibetan workers, he was able to eliminate the flooding problem.

Greatly impressed with the Austrian, Tenzin Gyatso asked Harrer to become his special tutor in 1950. Upon taking up his new duties, Harrer discovered that, although the Dalai Lama had some knowledge of world events outside his country, he did not know very much about the way these events fit together. With Harrer's help, the Dalai Lama dramatically improved his understanding of foreign affairs. Harrer also helped him learn to read English. These tutoring sessions continued until the Chinese invasion of Tibet forced Harrer to leave the country in 1951. Shortly thereafter, he wrote a book about his experiences, called *Seven Years in Tibet*.

who were in charge of the facilities. Attached to the monasteries were large estates that were worked by peasants. These people planted and harvested barley and other crops that were used to feed the residents of the monasteries. In addition to the monasteries, a small number of Tibetan aristocrats had large estates that were maintained by peasants. These aristocrats, along with Tibetan government officials and a few merchants, formed the upper classes. Making up another social division, similar to a middle class, were some independent Tibetan farmers who owned their land. The Dalai Lama's parents had been among this group. Below them on the social hierarchy was the large number of peasants who worked for someone else.

CHINESE INVASION

During the summer of 1950, Tibet was rocked by an earthquake that was centered near Chamdo, a city in eastern Tibet. Many people were killed and entire villages were destroyed. The shocks of the quake were felt for a great distance and even reached Lhasa, several hundred miles away. Several months later, the country was shaken by a different kind of tremor. Communists had taken control of China in 1949 and on October 7, 1950, some forty thousand Chinese troops began to advance into Tibet. They invaded from the north against Chamdo, and also from the south, to encircle the Tibetan troops. The Tibetan forces were almost immediately overwhelmed and had to surrender.

The Tibetan government asked for assistance from the United Nations as well as India and Great Britain. A few months earlier, in June 1950, when South Korea was invaded by Communist forces from North Korea, the United Nations had come to the aid of the South Koreans. Troops were sent to South Korea to drive back the North Korean invaders. However, the United Nations was far too focused on the situation in South Korea to deal with another crisis when Tibet made its appeal. For its part, the Indian government hoped that Tibet and China could work out their own problems peacefully. In the end, no country was willing to help defend Tibet against the onslaught of the massive Communist armies. The Tibetans themselves had little more than rifles to fight off the tanks and artillery of the Chinese forces.

As the Chinese advanced toward Lhasa, the Tibetan government debated about who should lead the nation through this crisis. The Dalai Lama was only sixteen years old at the time. He was not expected to take power until two years later. However, many people thought the time had come for him to take over political control of Tibet. Government leaders went to two state oracles—Gadong and Nechung—to ask for advice. Both agreed on the same course of action. As the Nechung Oracle told them: "The time has come. Make him king!" [25] The decision came as a shock to the Dalai Lama. As he recalled: "A month ago I had been a carefree young man eagerly looking forward to the annual opera festival. Now I was faced with the immediate prospect of leading my country as it prepared for war." [26]

Shortly after the visit to the oracle, as preparations for his investiture were under way, the Dalai Lama received a visit from his older brother, Takster Rinpoché, who told him a horrible story. For many years, Takster Rinpoché had been a monk at the monastery of Kumbum, and eventually, he became its abbot. Kumbum had been overrun by the Communists, who had held him there, essentially as a prisoner. After a time, they agreed to free him if he promised to convince his brother to let the Chinese take over the country. If the Dalai Lama did not agree, then Takster Rinpoché was expected to kill him. Of course, Takster Rinpoché did not carry out the instructions from his Chinese captors. Instead, he had decided to warn his brother about the Chinese and their hostile intentions.

Tenzin Gyatso had no intention of giving in to the Communists. On November 17, 1950, he formally took over political power in Tibet. He was given the Golden Wheel, which represented the Eightfold Path and served as a symbol of his power. But devout Buddhists do not believe in killing. Therefore, as their leader, he could not order his people to resist the Chinese invasion. Instead, he began to take diplomatic measures to deal with the situation. Since the time of the Great Fifth, two prime ministers had always carried on the day-to-day operations of the government. One was a monk, while the other was a lay politician. Tenzin Gyatso appointed the two prime ministers to officially run the country. Then he met with his cabinet and sent out ambassadors to several foreign countries, including the United States, to ask for aid. He also directed a team of diplomatic representatives to travel to China and try to bring a peaceful end to the conflict.

NECHUNG ORACLE

At the Nechung Monastery, Tibetans believe the important Buddhist god Dorje Drakden speaks through an individual known as an oracle. The Nechung Oracle first appeared in Tibet during the eighth century. The Second Dalai Lama consulted the oracle, and his successors continued this tradition. The oracle has also assisted Buddhist lamas in their search for the next reincarnation of the Dalai Lama. The current Dalai Lama has written that he consults the oracle to make important decisions. This does not mean that the oracle is the only source from which he seeks advice. However, he explains, "I seek his opinion in the same way as I seek the opinion of my Cabinet and just as I seek the opinion of my own conscience." He also added that the oracle's answers have frequently been right.*

When consulted by the Dalai Lama, the oracle dresses in a magnificent silk robe and wears an ornamented mirror on his chest. He also wears an elaborate piece of gear over his robe with flags and banners attached to it. To the music of horns and drums, he goes into a trance that gradually becomes deeper and deeper. His assistants place a heavy helmet on his head. Then the god enters his body. The oracle picks up a beautiful sword and starts to dance; the dance ends as he comes before the Dalai Lama and bows in front of him. The Dalai Lama then asks the oracle for advice, and the god Dorje Drakden answers through him. Finally, the oracle falls on the floor, worn out from his efforts.

* Source: Tenzin Gyatso, the Fourteenth Dalai Lama, *Freedom in Exile: The Autobiography of the Dalai Lama.* New York: HarperCollins, 1990, p. 212.

DEALING WITH THE COMMUNISTS

The Dalai Lama was urged by his advisors to leave Lhasa and head southward toward the Tibetan border with India. From there, he could slip into India, rather than be captured by the Chinese. He agreed. The Dalai Lama and his staff reached Dromo, near the border, in January 1951.

Meanwhile, the Tibetan delegation that had gone to China was forced by the Communists to sign an agreement. According to the so-called Seventeen-Point Agreement for the Peaceful Liberation of Tibet (see Appendix for full text), the Tibetan people had always been part of China. The Chinese had invaded Tibet to "liberate" the country from unspecified "imperialist forces" (presumably the Dalai Lama and his government) that had enslaved the Tibetan people. The document asserted that the Tibetan people had been reunited with "the big family of the People's Republic of China. . . ."

At this point, the Dalai Lama was receiving conflicting advice. Some advisors were urging him to flee to India. Others, however, were asking him to come back to Lhasa and lead the government under the authority of the Chinese. In July 1951, the Chinese, led by General Chiang Chin-wu, met with the Dalai Lama at Dromo. Tenzin Gyatso decided that he could deal with General Chiang. Under the terms of the Seventeen-Point Agreement, the Tibetans, as part of China, were to be given the right to local government. As a result, the Dalai Lama decided to return to Lhasa to run the government. He arrived there in August. As authors Roger Hicks and Ngakpa Chogyam wrote: "He did not want that responsibility, but he saw no alternative. . . . he was driven by two things: the sense of duty which any honorable man would feel in his position, and his vow as a Bodhisattva to work for the good of all . . . beings."[27]

Dealing with the conquerors, however, was not an easy task. The Chinese had placed thousands of troops in Tibet. Chinese generals then demanded that Tibetan farmers provide enough food to feed the invading soldiers. Tibetan aristocrats, who owned large estates, were forced to hand over both grain and money to the Chinese. Monasteries, which often owned large fields, were also required to provide the Chinese with surplus barley. However, there was not enough barley, potatoes, or other food to feed the Chinese soldiers. As a result, shortages began to develop in Tibet. The price of food increased rapidly, and the country was faced with the threat of famine.

Meanwhile, the Chinese began to indoctrinate Tibetans in the principles of communism. At the same time, the Tibetans began to resist the invaders. Children hurled stones at passing Chinese soldiers. Tibetans clapped when the Chinese marched by them. (This is a traditional way to drive out evil demons in Tibetan culture.) They also laughed at the Chinese and sang songs that poked fun at them. Although the invaders were upset by this behavior, they could do nothing to stop it. They asked the Tibetan prime ministers to step in and put an end to these activities.

During the Tibetan New Year celebrations, approximately one thousand protesters surrounded the house of a Chinese official in Lhasa. To deal with this problem, the Chinese moved more troops into Lhasa. Finally, they put pressure on the Dalai Lama to fire his two prime ministers, who were popular with the Tibetan people because they resisted the Chinese. The ministers were forced to resign in 1952. In the meantime, the Chinese were setting up their own administration to run the country without the input of the Dalai Lama. Some Tibetan political leaders abandoned the Dalai Lama and chose to work for the Communists. Those who refused to support the Chinese had their lands taken from them.

VISITING CHINA

In 1954, the Dalai Lama was invited by the Communist government to visit China. Some of his advisors warned him that if he went to the Chinese capital at Beijing, he might be imprisoned there. Despite the danger, the Dalai Lama decided that a face-to-face meeting with Chinese leader Mao Zedong might improve relations between the two countries. Tibet had few roads at the time, so the 2,000-mile (3,219-kilometer) journey took several weeks.

In the first meetings between the two leaders, Communist Chairman Mao assured the Dalai Lama that Tibet would be permitted to move at its own pace in adopting the ways of the Communists. He emphasized that the Chinese only wanted to help the Tibetans become a more modern country. At first, the Dalai Lama was encouraged by these words.

His attitude soon changed, however. In a final meeting with Mao Zedong, the Chinese leader told the Dalai Lama: "Your attitude is good, you know. Religion is poison. Firstly it reduces the population, because monks and nuns stay celibate, and secondly it neglects material progress." As the Dalai Lama later wrote: "At this I felt a violent burning sensation all over my face and I was suddenly very afraid. 'So,' I thought, 'you are the destroyer of the *Dharma* after all.'"[28]

REVOLT IN TIBET

As the Dalai Lama returned to Tibet in 1955, conditions in the country were growing worse. The Chinese were trying to turn the Tibetan peasants against the aristocrats and Buddhist monks. Communist leaders encouraged the peasants to accuse the landowners and Buddhist lamas of exploiting them by controlling the land. Most peasants, however, were strong believers in Buddhism and continued to respect the lamas. In eastern Tibet, the Chinese were forcing farmers off their lands and onto large collective farms. Communist leaders also took over the lands controlled by the monasteries. As a result, monks were no longer able to grow enough food to feed themselves, and many had to leave the monasteries. In addition, nomads, who owned herds of yaks, were being driven by the Communists to give up their independent way of life and move onto the collective farms.

The Tibetans resisted these changes and began to attack the Chinese. Some of the rebels took refuge in Chantrent Sampheling Monastery in Kham. The monastery was bombed by a Chinese airplane and destroyed. Another revolt broke out in Lithang. This time, the rebels took refuge at Lithang Monastery, and it, too, was destroyed by the Chinese. Monks were arrested and imprisoned, and many of them died.

These attacks angered the Tibetans. When news of the bombings of the monasteries reached the central part of the country, rebellion, which had been limited there before, began to spread to this area. In 1956, a group called Mimang Tsongdu put up posters in Lhasa criticizing the Chinese administration. Mimang Tsongdu called for the Dalai Lama to take control of the government. Eventually, the leaders of this group were rounded up by the Chinese and put into prison.

Meanwhile, Chairman Mao had directed that a "Preparatory Committee for the Tibet Autonomous Region" should govern the country under the direction of the Dalai Lama, who agreed to head the committee. However, the Dalai Lama soon realized that the group would have no real power. Most of the people selected to serve on it were either Communists or Tibetans who supported the Chinese.

CONFLICT INCREASES

In 1956, the Dalai Lama was invited to India to celebrate the twenty-five-hundredth anniversary of the year that the Buddha achieved enlightenment. During his visit, he met with Prime Minister Jawaharlal Nehru of India. The Dalai Lama told Nehru about the revolt in Tibet. If he was hoping for support from the Indian leader, Tenzin Gyatso was disappointed. Nehru suggested that the Dalai Lama return to Tibet and cooperate with the Chinese. At this time, the Dalai Lama was considering the possibility of remaining in India. Nehru dissuaded him, saying that he could do far more good for his people by returning to Tibet.

While in India, the Dalai Lama also met Zhou Enlai, the Chinese premier. The premier admitted that the Chinese had made mistakes in Tibet. He assured the Dalai Lama that the Chinese would now begin to handle the situation in Tibet differently, and that conditions would improve very soon. Like Nehru, Zhou Enlai tried to convince the Dalai Lama to return to Tibet.

Despite Zhou's promises, when the Dalai Lama returned to Lhasa in 1957, the conflict was growing. Monasteries were being ruined. Men suspected of assisting the rebels were being shot without trial. In the eastern and central provinces, Tibetan guerrillas were attacking Chinese military posts. "They even tried to secure my approval for what they were doing," the Dalai Lama wrote. "Alas I could not give it, even though as a young man and a patriot I had some thought now to do so."[29]

The Chinese met with the Tibetan cabinet and told its members that they had to do something to stop the uprising. The Chinese even wanted the small Tibetan Army sent out to stop the guerrillas. The cabinet, however, defied the Chinese and would not do what they ordered. Meanwhile, the Chinese were suffering increasing casualties in their battles against the Tibetan guerrillas. At the same time, more and more refugees were fleeing the countryside to seek protection in the capital city of Lhasa.

EXILE IN INDIA

In March 1959, the Chinese leaders asked the Dalai Lama to attend a special dance performance that was being staged at their headquarters in Lhasa. When word of this invitation leaked out to the people in Lhasa, they were afraid that the Dalai Lama would be taken hostage. On the morning of March 10, a mass of people surrounded the Summer Palace, where the Dalai Lama was living. The crowds were so large that it was impossible for him to exit the building to attend the event at Chinese headquarters.

The Dalai Lama was afraid that the situation might grow worse, and that the Chinese might begin to fire on the crowds of protesters. Letters were sent back and forth between the Dalai Lama and the Chinese officials. Still, the situation remained tense. On March 17, the Chinese began to fire artillery at the Summer Palace. By this time, the Dalai Lama realized that he had to leave the country; it was no longer safe for him to remain in Tibet. That evening, Tenzin Gyatso disguised himself as a Tibetan soldier. Then he left the palace. Behind him, members of his staff also made their escape so they could help the Dalai Lama carry on the government in exile.

They slipped out of Lhasa, evading the Chinese, and joined Tibetan guerrillas outside the city. Then they headed south along snow-covered paths and across the mountains. At one point, an "old man joined the party as they were climbing, and seeing how His Holiness's pony was flagging, he made him a present of a pure white horse. The man's name was Tashi Norbu, or Auspicious Jewel, an old man who appeared from nowhere." [30]

In southern Tibet, the Dalai Lama began to set up a new government. He and his staff, however, were afraid that they might be followed by Chinese army units. Although the weather was extremely cold, the Dalai Lama continued to travel southward. He and his entourage reached India in early April, where the Dalai Lama was given protection by the Indian government of Nehru, who had agreed to allow the Dalai Lama and his party to take up residence in India.

6

Leader in Exile

Everything is changeable,
everything appears and disappears;
there is no blissful peace until one passes
beyond the agony of life and death.

—The Buddha

When the Dalai Lama arrived at Bomdila in northern India, he was very sick. He was suffering from an illness called dysentery. Caused by bacteria, dysentery produces stomach cramps, bleeding, and diarrhea. The Dalai Lama was treated for his disease, and eventually was able to move to a town in northwest India called Mussoorie.

As he traveled along the way, many Buddhists turned out to see their spiritual leader, proclaiming, "Hail to the Dalai Lama! Long live the Dalai Lama!"[31] Meanwhile, in Lhasa, Tibetans who had taken part in the mass demonstration outside the Summer Palace were arrested. Most men were removed from the city by the Chinese and taken to other parts of Tibet so they could no longer participate in the revolt. This effectively put an end to the uprising. Without the leadership of the Dalai Lama, the Chinese were able to secure total control of Tibet.

In April, the Dalai Lama met with Indian Prime Minister Nehru. Although the Indian government was willing to let the Dalai Lama give a press conference, Nehru did not want him to say anything that would be interpreted as overly critical of China. The Indian prime minister was in a difficult position. He sympathized with the Dalai Lama, yet India wanted to retain peace with its powerful Chinese neighbor. Therefore, Nehru asked that the Dalai Lama refrain from saying too much about the struggle for Tibetan independence or the Chinese killings of Tibetans in Lhasa. Following the press conference, Nehru issued a statement in which he refused to recognize the Dalai Lama's new government in exile as the legitimate government of Tibet.

As the situation in Tibet grew worse, some people began to escape from the country. By the fall of 1959, thirty thousand Tibetans had already fled to India. New jobs and homes had to be found for these people. The Indian government set up refugee camps, but these were often located in hot, humid areas. The Tibetans were not used to this type of climate, and many became ill. After the Dalai Lama discussed this problem with Nehru, the Indian government moved the Tibetan refugees to a different location. India also provided many of the refugees with jobs building roads in the northern part of the country.

GOVERNMENT IN DHARAMSALA

In April 1960, the Dalai Lama moved his government to Dharamsala in northwestern India, which became known as "Little Lhasa," the location of the Tibetan government in exile. India provided the land and a home for the Dalai Lama. The government included not only the Dalai Lama and the cabinet, or Kashag, but also an assembly elected by refugees from the major areas of Tibet. (This official body replaced the much larger elected assembly that had helped govern Tibet in the past when the country was still independent.) India provided guards to protect the Dalai Lama and his government officials.

Another problem that faced the Dalai Lama was helping the Tibetan children who came into India. Some of them were

VISITING THE CAMPS

In his autobiography, *Freedom in Exile,* the Dalai Lama described what he saw during his regular visits to the Tibetan refugee camps in India:

> Often I had to console the refugees in their sadness when I visited these camps. The thought of being so far from home and with no prospect of seeing ice or snow, let alone our beloved mountains, was hard for them to bear. I tried to take their minds off the past. Instead, I told them that the future of Tibet depended on us refugees. If we wanted to preserve our culture and way of life, the only way to do so was by building strong communities. I spoke too of the importance of education and even of the significance of the institution of marriage. Although it was not really a proper thing for a monk to advise, I told the women that wherever possible they should marry Tibetan men so that the children they bore would be Tibetans too.*

* Source: Tenzin Gyatso, the Fourteenth Dalai Lama, *Freedom in Exile: The Autobiography of the Dalai Lama*. New York: HarperCollins, 1990, p. 171.

orphans who had lost their parents during the escape from Tibet. In Dharamsala, the government established the Nursery for Tibetan Refugee Children. By the end of 1960, approximately five hundred children were enrolled in the nursery school program. Over the next few decades, this program expanded to include nurseries in Tibetan settlements throughout India. They became part of the Tibetan Children's Village, which even today continues to serve several thousand children every year. In addition to these facilities, the Indian government provided financial assistance to help the Dalai Lama set up education programs for older Tibetan children. Their purpose was to help preserve Tibet's culture and language.

Financial aid for the Dalai Lama's government came not only from India, but also from other governments. In addition, the Tibetan government raised money from charitable funds and wealthy individuals who wanted to assist the Dalai Lama. The Dalai Lama himself provided a great deal of financial support for government programs. Over the years, he had received many gifts from devout Buddhists in Tibet and had success-fully taken some of this money out of the country before the Communist takeover. He used it to finance social programs for Tibetans in India.

March 10 had become an important date in the history of Tibet. This was the day that the massive demonstration had occurred outside the Dalai Lama's Summer Palace in Lhasa. Beginning in 1960, the Dalai Lama would make an annual speech on the anniversary of the Tibetan "People's Uprising." He recalled:

> On this first occasion, I stressed the need for my people to take a long-term view of the situation in Tibet. For those of us in exile, I said that our priority must be resettlement and the continuity of our cultural traditions. As to the future, I stated my belief that, with Truth, Justice and Courage as our weapons, we Tibetans would eventually prevail in regaining freedom for Tibet.[32]

As a way of preserving their spiritual traditions, Buddhist monks who fled Tibet established new monasteries in India. They often obtained the money to build these monasteries by begging among the Buddhists of India. Several monasteries were built in the southern part of India. Nechung Monastery, for example, was located near the Dalai Lama's home in Dharamsala. The original Nechung Monastery had been at Lhasa before the Dalai Lama had fled from Tibet.

As another way of preserving Tibetan culture, the government in exile established the Library of Tibetan Works and Archives. As Tibetans fled their homes, they brought their books of Buddhist teachings with them. These were preserved at the library. In addition, the library publishes new books on Buddhism.

COMMUNICATING HIS MESSAGE

During the 1960s, the Dalai Lama traveled throughout India, visiting the new communities of Tibetans. Beginning in 1967, he also began to journey abroad. His first trip took him to Japan and Thailand, two important centers of Buddhism. As the Buddhist tradition spread outward from India, it gained many followers throughout Southeast Asia. Both schools of Buddhism—Theravada and Mahayana—can be found in these areas.

In 1973, the Dalai Lama went to Europe. Stops on his trip included Holland, Sweden, Denmark, and Great Britain. He had a visit with the Roman Catholic pope in Rome. He also traveled to Switzerland, where some two hundred Tibetan orphans had been adopted by Swiss families during the 1960s. Then, in 1979, the Dalai Lama toured the United States. He spoke about Buddhism as well as the plight of Tibet.

Meanwhile, the situation in China had begun to change. In 1976, Mao Zedong died, and his closest associates were soon replaced as leaders of the Chinese government. In 1977, one of the new Chinese leaders issued a statement calling on the Dalai Lama to return to Tibet, along with his government. The following year, the Chinese released the Panchen Lama from prison. He had been put behind bars approximately ten years earlier for publicly supporting the Dalai Lama inside Tibet. Rather than flee with the rest of the government, the Panchen Lama had stayed behind to deal as best he could with the Chinese. The Chinese tried to force him to take over the Dalai Lama's position, but he refused. Aside from his imprisonment, he had also been brutally tortured. Now, as relations in Asia seemed to be gradually improving, China suddenly agreed to set him free. About the same time, the Chinese also released other members of the Tibetan government who had been unable to escape to India.

The Dalai Lama proposed to the Chinese that he send a fact-finding mission to Tibet to investigate the conditions among the Tibetan people living under communism. The Chinese agreed, because they thought the team would make a good report. They also wanted the Dalai Lama to return to Tibet and run the country under their guidance and control. In August 1979, the Dalai Lama's team traveled to Beijing and from there to Tibet. Among its members was the Dalai Lama's brother Lobsang Samten. The team was accompanied to Tibet by Chinese officials, who wanted to control what they saw. However, news of the team's arrival had leaked out, and its members were met by large crowds of cheering Tibetans. The Chinese were surprised by the enormous support that the Tibetans showed for the Dalai Lama.

What the fact-finding team learned from the Tibetan people was not encouraging. As the Dalai Lama wrote, the team delegates received "numberless accounts of years of famine, mass starvation, public execution . . . and violations of human rights . . . which included the abduction of children into forced labor gangs . . . the imprisonment of innocent citizens and the deaths of thousands of monks and nuns in concentration camps."[33]

Additional teams were sent to Tibet in 1980. They, too, were warmly greeted by the Tibetans, who wanted news of the Dalai Lama. One of the teams investigated the educational system for

Tibetans under Chinese rule. Like that of the original team, its report was quite negative because Tibetan children were being indoctrinated in the principles of communism. Although the Chinese continued to encourage the Dalai Lama to return to Tibet, he realized that as long as the Chinese were in control, he would never be allowed to run the government in the best interest of the Tibetan people.

7

Tibet Under Communism

At every stage along the journey, my forced optimism was dealt fresh blows by the news and reports . . . that the situation throughout Tibet was rapidly slipping . . . from my [control].

— Tenzin Gyatso, the Fourteenth Dalai Lama

W hat the Dalai Lama's fact-finding teams saw in Tibet had been the result of twenty years of harsh Communist rule. While he was still in Tibet, the Dalai Lama had been a strong force that prevented the Chinese from making drastic changes. Once he left, the Communists began to do whatever they wanted, causing tremendous disruptions in the lives of the Tibetan people.

The process of collectivization increased. Large estate owners lost their lands. For a short period, these lands were handed over to the peasants who had previously worked them for wealthy Tibetans. Then the farms were taken away from the peasants, too, and turned into large collectives. The Communists

LIFE ON THE COMMUNE

According to historian Warren Smith, Tibetan peasants who worked on communes received a fixed amount, or ration, of food each day for their labor:

> Work points, which enabled Tibetans to buy their own grain from the Chinese, were awarded at the rate of 10 *karma* per day for officials . . . 8 *karma* per day for the most diligent laborers, 5 to 7 for the less diligent, 4 *karma* for shepherds and 2 to 3 *karma* for old people who worked and children below age 14. Old people unable to work and children too young to work got no *karma* and no ration; they were expected to be supported by their families on their own inadequate ration. 10 *karma* per day enabled a worker to receive a ration . . . of grain and . . . butter . . . barely a subsistence ration. . . . The Chinese justified the sacrifice and hardship as necessary to reach the socialist paradise, an era that would bring unbounded happiness and prosperity.*

Unfortunately, the Chinese themselves had made the process more difficult for Tibetans. They forced the peasants to grow wheat instead of barley. Wheat did not grow well in the rainy and cold climate of Tibet. As a result, food shortages actually increased.

* Source: Warren Smith, Jr., *Tibetan Nation*. Boulder, CO: Westview Press, 1996, p. 552.

forced the Tibetan farmers to form Mutual Aid Teams. These were labor groups that planted and harvested the crops. Mutual Aid Teams were also put to work digging irrigation ditches to bring water to the farms, as well as clearing new farmland. The Chinese wanted to expand the number of acres being cultivated so that there would be more food available for their occupying soldiers.

Buddhist monks were forced to leave their monasteries and participate in some of these agricultural projects. With the Dalai Lama gone from Tibet, the Communists began to reduce the number of monks in the country and to close the temples and monasteries. The number of monks fell from 114,000 in 1958 to 18,000 in 1960. In that same time period, the number of temples and monasteries in Tibet dropped from 2,700 to 370.[34] The Chinese wanted to replace Buddhism as the religion of Tibet with the ideology of communism, which did not accept organized religion.

As part of this program, Tibetans were required to participate in "study groups." They studied the teachings of Mao and the other main thinkers in the Communist tradition. Study group members were expected to make sure that everyone enthusiastically supported communism. They were expected to report to the Chinese authorities anyone who did not seem to be a true believer in Communist doctrine. As a result, family members were pressured to inform on one another if they suspected that a relative did not support communism. They were also expected to criticize the Dalai Lama publicly.

These policies were designed by the Communists to break down family units and destroy traditional Buddhist values. One of the programs instituted by the Communists was called "Destroy the Four Pests." The so-called "four pests" were rats, mice, flies, and sparrows. The campaign tried to force Tibetans to engage in a widespread extermination of these creatures. Buddhism is opposed to the destruction of any form of life. Thus, the campaign was another brazen attempt to undermine the Tibetans' Buddhist beliefs.

Any Tibetans who did not participate in the required Communist programs were sent off to prisons or labor camps. At some of these camps, prisoners were forced to work in mines or build large dams. Over the three decades between 1949 and 1979, an estimated 173,000 Tibetans died from being tortured in these prisons and labor camps. Almost 157,000 Tibetans were executed by the Communists, while another 343,000 died of starvation.[35]

CHINESE POLICIES

In 1964, the Chinese set up the Tibet Autonomous Region (TAR). They announced that adults would now be free to vote for a Tibetan People's Congress that would help govern the country. This act was supposed to demonstrate that Tibetans were now capable of governing themselves. However, the selection of candidates who would run for Congress as well as the elections themselves were tightly controlled by the Communists.

But the situation inside Tibet would grow even worse. In 1966, Chairman Mao launched the Cultural Revolution in China. This movement was aimed at purifying communism by eliminating all politicians and ideas that did not support Mao. The Cultural Revolution was spearheaded by students, called Red Guards. They were ordered to attack officials who were suspected of not being loyal Communists. As a result, a wave of violence swept across China.

The violence of the Cultural Revolution also came to Tibet. Red Guards attacked monasteries and temples, including Jokhang in Lhasa. Priceless Buddhist religious articles were taken, and the temples themselves were destroyed. Tibetans were ordered to turn over their own religious books and other items to the Red Guards. To show their support for Mao, the residents of Lhasa were required to display pictures of the chairman on their houses.

At the same time, Tibetans continued to suffer from food shortages. The process of collectivization had not succeeded in feeding both the Tibetans and the Chinese soldiers. As a result, a revolt began in the western part of Tibet during 1968. It was led by a woman named Nyemo Ani. The rebellion grew, and in

1969, the Communists brought in more troops to put down the uprising. Nyemo Ani was captured and executed, along with others who had publicly opposed the Chinese government.

THE PLIGHT OF TIBET

After the Dalai Lama fled Lhasa and set up a new government in India, he tried to publicize the brutal conditions that existed inside his native country. However, his efforts seemed to have little impact. During the 1970s, the United States established diplomatic relations with China, and trade with the Chinese was gradually expanded. The U.S. government also recognized the right of the Chinese to control Tibet. Meanwhile, the Chinese government in Tibet launched another attack on the Dalai Lama, who was accused of encouraging his followers to commit murders. By the early 1970s, only eight Buddhist monasteries remained in Tibet, and the number of monks had been reduced to about one thousand.[36]

The Chinese had made every effort to stamp out Buddhism inside Tibet. As a result, at the end of the 1970s they were surprised to learn that their policies had not been entirely successful when crowds of Tibetans turned out to greet the Dalai Lama's fact-finding team. The Chinese realized that their programs had not worked, and that the time had come to change them.

During the early 1980s, the number of collective farms began to be reduced. Tibetans were given their own land and permitted to tend their own herds. They were also encouraged to publicly express their religious beliefs and worship in Buddhist temples. As a result, Tibetans began to rebuild monasteries, religious shrines, and temples that had been destroyed during the Cultural Revolution. The government also agreed to reconstruct some of the monasteries that had been damaged. The number of people worshiping in the temples increased tremendously. An estimated ninety thousand Tibetans came to Jokhang Temple each month. Tibetans also began to send their children to monasteries to be educated by monks. In the past, children had only been allowed to attend schools controlled by the Communists.

By 1983, however, the Communists realized that they might have gone too far. Buddhism, which was an essential element of life inside Tibet, had begun to flourish again. Immediately, the Chinese clamped down. They limited the amount of money Tibetans were permitted to donate to support temples and monasteries. In addition, the Communist government established "democratic management committees" inside the monasteries. These committees were ordered to expose any monks who were opposed to communism and to provide their names to Chinese officials.

Tibetan affairs expert Elizabeth Napper told the Senate Foreign Relations Committee that she had worked with Buddhist nuns who had been driven out of Tibet. Many of these nuns, according to Napper, supported Tibetan independence. They waved the Tibetan flag or carried signs that said: LONG LIVE THE DALAI LAMA. These nuns were arrested by the Chinese and beaten. According to Napper:

> The beatings start in the vehicle on the way to the police station and continue through an interrogation that can take place over several days. Various instruments of torture are routinely used such as electric cattle prods . . . electric shocks that knock a person across the room, described by one nun as "a pain that pierced the heart," another called "the airplane" in which the arms are tied behind the body and then the rope is put over something hung from the ceiling so that the person is pulled up in such a way that shoulders are often dislocated.[37]

After their torture, the nuns were routinely thrown into prisons without any trials. They remained there for several years before being released. Afterward, some of these nuns fled Tibet and made their way to Dharamsala, the headquarters of the Tibetan government in exile.

CONFLICT INSIDE TIBET

Meanwhile, the Dalai Lama's speeches and trips to the United States helped focus the attention of Americans on conditions inside Tibet. In 1987, the U.S. Congress passed a resolution that stated that the Chinese had invaded the country in 1950 and "exercised dominion over the Tibetan people, who always considered themselves as independent, through the presence of a large occupation force." This resolution, however, had no impact on the official policy of the U.S. government. Although the United States publicly condemned suspected Chinese abuses of human rights in Tibet, the Americans continued to hold to the assertion that Tibet is a legitimate part of China.

In September 1987, the Dalai Lama presented a new "Five-Point Peace Plan" to a group of American congressional representatives (see Appendix for full text). This included: "Transformation of the whole of Tibet into a zone of peace" and "Respect for the Tibetan people's fundamental human rights and democratic freedoms," as well as "Commencement of earnest negotiations on the future status of Tibet and relations between the Tibetan and Chinese peoples." However, the Dalai Lama's program was immediately rejected by the Chinese, who subsequently used violence to put down demonstrations by supporters of the spiritual leader's plan.

While the Dalai Lama was in the United States, the Chinese executed two men whom Tibetans regarded as freedom fighters. A small demonstration, mainly carried out by Buddhist monks, occurred in Lhasa to protest the executions. The protesters were immediately arrested. This led to a larger demonstration in October 1987 and more arrests. The following March, when Buddhist monks in Lhasa protested the arrest of a college professor who had opposed government policies, police who were trying to end the demonstration used clubs and even electric cattle prods. By the time the incident came to an end, at least twelve monks had been killed.

Later in 1988, the Dalai Lama made a new proposal during a speech in Strasbourg, France. It called for Tibet to "become a self-governing democratic political entity founded on law by agreement of the people . . . in association with the People's Republic of China. The Government of the People's Republic of China could be responsible for Tibet's foreign policy." This "middle-way" proposal would have given Tibet control of its local affairs, while the country continued to be associated with China. The Dalai Lama reiterated that Tibet had always been independent and never considered itself a part of China. However, he admitted that in the past, Tibet had sometimes developed associations with powerful empires, such as the Mongols and Chinese.

The Communists rejected this proposal, just as they had the earlier one the Dalai Lama had presented. In December 1988, a small demonstration by monks occurred in Lhasa. The Chinese tried to break up the protest, killing and wounding several demonstrators. This led to larger demonstrations and riots in March 1989. Once again, the Chinese stepped in and between 80 and 150 Tibetans were killed.

The conflict in Tibet was growing much worse.

8

Citizen of
the World

Whenever I meet even a "foreigner,"
I have always the same feeling:
"I am meeting another member of the human family."
This attitude has deepened my affection
and respect for all beings.

— Tenzin Gyatso, the Fourteenth Dalai Lama

I n 1989, the Dalai Lama was awarded the Nobel Peace Prize. In giving him the award, the Nobel Committee mentioned the Dalai Lama's commitment to "peaceful solutions based upon tolerance and mutual respect in order to preserve the historical and cultural heritage of his people."

U.S. President George H.W. Bush met with the Dalai Lama in 1991. That same year, the American president delivered an address to Congress in which he referred to Tibet as "a nation under foreign occupation." Nevertheless, the official position of the United States did not change. As the Department of State put it: "The United States, like all other governments throughout the world, considers Tibet to be a part of China. . . . No country recognizes Tibet as independent of China. The United States has never taken the position that Tibet is an independent country, nor has it recognized the Dalai Lama as the leader of a government in exile."[38]

Meanwhile, the Chinese government stepped up its propaganda campaign against the Dalai Lama. Within Tibet, people were expected to demonstrate their opposition to the Dalai Lama to satisfy the Communist government. In 1989, the Panchen Lama, the second highest ranking leader of Tibetan Buddhism, died. Traditionally, his reincarnation is discovered by a search team sent out by the Dalai Lama. However, the Tibetan Communist government selected its own replacement for the Panchen Lama. Tibetan Buddhists had compiled a list of potential successors over a period of many years, and it was from this list that Gedhun Choekyi Nyima was chosen and recognized as the true incarnation of the previous Panchen Lama. The Chinese did not accept the new Panchen Lama chosen by the Tibetans. Instead, the Communist government increased its efforts to criticize the Dalai Lama and reduce his influence in Tibet.

PURSUING THE MIDDLE WAY

From his home in India, the Dalai Lama continued to search for a compromise with the Communists. In a speech delivered to the

British Parliament in 1996, the Dalai Lama said:

> Historically and according to international law Tibet is an
> independent country under Chinese occupation. However, . . .
> I have adopted a "middle-way" approach of reconciliation and
> compromise in the pursuit of a peaceful and negotiated reso-
> lution of the Tibetan issue. While it is the overwhelming desire
> of the Tibetan people to regain their national independence, I
> have repeatedly and publicly stated that I am willing to enter
> into negotiations on the basis of an agenda that does not
> include independence.[39]

Once again, the Dalai Lama called for an association between
Tibet and China that would allow Tibetans to run their own
local government, while China remained in control of foreign
affairs. (This "middle-way" approach reflected the Buddhist
ideal of finding a middle path between completely denying life's
pleasures and enjoying them to excess. The Buddha himself
had defined this path over two thousand years earlier.)

Nevertheless, the Chinese refused to negotiate with the Dalai
Lama. In 1997, the Dalai Lama once again called on the Chinese
to enter into negotiations. As he put it:

> In human societies there will always be differences of views
> and interests. But the reality today is that we are interdependent
> and have to co-exist on this small planet. Therefore, the only
> sensible and intelligent way of resolving differences and clashes
> of interests, whether between individuals or nations, is through
> dialogue. . . . With these convictions, I have led the Tibetan
> freedom struggle on a path of nonviolence, and have sought
> a mutually agreeable solution to the Tibetan issue through
> negotiations in a spirit of reconciliation and compromise.[40]

As the Dalai Lama pointed out, his approach arose from the
spirit of Buddhism, which emphasizes the interdependence of all
people and a dedication to nonviolence.

However, the Chinese still refused to negotiate with the Dalai
Lama. As he reported, they resorted to a policy of "expulsion,

imprisonment and death" for Tibetans who disagreed with their policies.[41] By the end of the 1990s, an estimated two hundred thousand Tibetans had been exiled from the country. They were living in the countries of Nepal, India, and Bhutan. The Dalai Lama's government also reported that more than one million Tibetans had been killed by the Chinese. However, the Chinese government denied this.

CONDITIONS INSIDE TIBET

Reports coming out of Tibet in 2000 indicated that the Chinese government was indeed imposing harsh conditions on the people. In testimony before Congress, one expert stated that the Chinese had a large number of troops stationed outside the Tibetan capital of Lhasa. These forces were intended to "both intimidate the local Tibetan population and make the Chinese settler population feel secure."[42]

In addition, the Chinese were moving settlers out of China and into the Tibetan cities and countryside. China claimed that only about 500,000 Chinese had been settled in Tibet. The Dalai Lama's government claimed that this figure was much higher, at about 7.5 million settlers. In fact, the Dalai Lama was fearful that the Chinese were trying to become the majority population of Tibet and turn native Tibetans into a minority in their own land.

REMAKING TIBET

In 2001, the Dalai Lama repeated his claims that Tibet has been turned into a totalitarian society by the Chinese government:

> I have always said that if the majority of Tibetans in Tibet were truly satisfied with the state of affairs in Tibet I would have no reason, no justification and no desire to raise my voice against the situation in Tibet. Sadly, whenever Tibetans speak up . . . they are arrested, imprisoned and labeled as counter-revolutionaries. They have no opportunity and no freedom to speak out the truth.[43]

Today, although many Tibetans still lack freedom, other conditions inside Tibet may have improved. According to author Lewis Simons, writing in 2002 about his recent visit to Tibet, the Chinese have been trying to modernize the country. Immigrants from China and Mongolia, along with Tibetans themselves, have been put to work building roads. Chinese immigrants are setting up shops, hotels, and restaurants in Tibetan towns. In addition, the Chinese have built schools, hospitals, airports, and even a Tibetan railroad.

At the same time, however, the Chinese have also continued their attacks on Buddhism. Indeed, the number of monks has been cut by two-thirds. Even so, many Tibetans in the countryside continue to worship at Buddhist shrines and temples. In short, according to Simons, the Chinese seem to have recognized that they cannot eliminate all the traditions of Tibet.[44] The ideals and values of Buddhism, as well as the influence of the Dalai Lama, are simply too strong.

9

Thoughts of the Dalai Lama

I believe that the very purpose of life is to be happy.
From the very core of our being, we desire contentment.
In my own limited experience I have found that
the more we care for the happiness of others,
the greater is our own sense of well-being.

—Tenzin Gyatso, the Fourteenth Dalai Lama

Compassion is at the center of Buddhist teachings. The Buddha's compassion enabled him to reach a state of enlightenment, and he wanted others to possess the same amount of compassion.

"Love and compassion are common to all faith traditions," said the Dalai Lama during a trip to the United States in 2001.

> Compassion for all sentient [conscious] beings made by your Creator, this is integral to Christianity. Christians strive to fulfill the wishes of your Creator, and the primary wish of your Creator is love, is that not so? The Buddha and the Christ were similar men: ascetics, men used to hardship and not to luxury, men of perseverance and effort, extraordinary teachers.[45]

In his book *Awakening the Mind, Lightening the Heart: Core Teachings of Tibetan Buddhism,* the Dalai Lama wrote that the awakening mind filled with love "is the root of all happiness and peace in the entire universe."[46] The Dalai Lama recommended that people begin to achieve happiness and peace by reciting the following poem:

> *I take refuge in the Buddha, Dharma, and spiritual community*
>   *[the Three Jewels of Buddhism]*
> *Until I attain the state of enlightenment.*
> *By the force of generosity and other virtues,*
> *May I achieve Buddhahood to benefit all sentient beings.*[47]

Buddhists generally recite this verse three times. Each time, they think about its meaning—to devote themselves to the Three Jewels of Buddhism and to help other people. Both of these goals are very important. People who are dedicated to the Three Jewels only for themselves and not in order to help others are not truly practicing Buddhism.

After reciting the poem and thinking about what it means, Buddhists begin to say prayers and to meditate. In his book, the Dalai Lama emphasized that it is not enough to go through the motions of Buddhism. That is, going to a temple and praying are not enough to make someone a devout

Buddhist. An individual's mind must be enlightened—that is, open to the needs of others and dedicated to fulfilling those needs. Instead of holding anger toward another person, the heart should be filled with love. This attitude helps others, too. "When we can help others generate virtue in their hearts, make them happy and their lives meaningful, that is a true service to the Buddha and his doctrine," wrote the Dalai Lama. "We need to be diligent and direct our best efforts this way. That, I believe, is how to fulfill the other's welfare as well as one's own."[48]

Achieving these goals takes study and effort. It is easy to feel angry with other people, especially if they seem to have wronged us. It is also easy to form strong attachments to material things—money, clothes, and toys, to name just a few. But these things, according to Buddhism, do not bring enlightenment. They only stand in the way. Through prayer, meditation, and study, we can eliminate the attachment to material things from our hearts and minds.

"THE RAYS OF THE SUN"
Many of the ideals of Buddhism are contained in a poem titled "The Rays of the Sun," written during the fifteenth century. It begins:

> *Arising from the source of love and compassion*
> *The ship of the awakening mind is well launched.*

The Buddha himself set down eighty-four thousand teachings to help his followers eliminate bad feelings so they could experience compassion. His instructions are called *nectar*. In the ancient Indian language Sanskrit, *nectar* means "that which grants immortality." Following the teachings of the Buddha helps his followers achieve nirvana.

These teachings also help Buddhists overcome misfortune and turn it into a positive force in their lives. For example, the Dalai Lama has written that the invasion of Tibet by the Chinese forced him to come into contact with the outside world. Before the invasion, he had lived cut off from the world, spending much of his time cloistered in Potala Palace. The Chinese invasion first forced him into exile. Then, his devotion to his country required him to travel around the world to speak out about Tibet and Buddhism to others. As a result, Tibetan Buddhism has become much more widely known.

MEDITATION

Mind training through meditation is the key to adopting the values and teachings of Buddhism. Buddhists believe that most unhappiness comes from inside our own minds—that is, from our own view of events. If we train our minds to see many of these events in a positive way, we can begin to achieve happiness. Meditation is the way Buddhists train their minds to practice the principles of their religion. Tibetan Buddhists meditate in the presence of pictures or images, including the Buddha as well as the bodhisattva Avalokiteshvara. According to the Dalai Lama, these images help Buddhists to follow the teachings of their religion throughout the day. Buddhists also make offerings to these images, such as food and flowers. Then they sit on a cushion or in a chair to meditate. During meditation, an individual may focus on a specific value, such as love. For example, he or she might think, "May all sentient beings be free from suffering."

Buddhists are then encouraged to think about the Three Jewels and how they can help them achieve eventual nirvana. The Dalai Lama has urged Buddhists to repeat the poem about taking refuge in the Three Jewels, while visualizing other people and your compassion for them. Buddhists see all human beings as interdependent—relying on one another to achieve happiness. Therefore, what one person does directly affects others. If an individual acts with compassion toward others, this brings more love to the world and removes hatred.

Buddhists often meditate with the help of a spiritual master. This person should practice the teachings of the Buddha, thoroughly understand Buddhist principles, and be an inspired teacher. When they meditate alone, Buddhists visualize their spiritual master to help them focus their minds. "At the end of the meditation session, however long or short it has been, it is very important to rejoice in what you have done," wrote the Dalai Lama.

> Think that all the positive potential you have accumulated during the session is not directed to your own personal gain but only to the welfare of other sentient beings. . . . You should not be like an actor, who puts on a costume for the performance and takes it off immediately at the end. Many of us are like that. Although we undertake the practice very seriously during the meditation session, after it is over, we revert to the same negative person again. We do whatever we like—fighting, quarreling, and so forth. You should neither think nor behave like that. Things are easy during the actual meditation session because there is no one to interfere with you. But once you emerge from your session, you will encounter many external conditions that may harm your practice. . . . Meditation is like recharging your battery. During the actual session you are recharged, but the purpose of recharging your battery is to put it to use.[49]

UNDERSTANDING LIFE

To help them in practicing the purpose of meditation, Buddhists focus on the realities of life. Among these is the fact that human beings have far more potential than other creatures to bring love and compassion to the world. Humans must use this potential to its fullest. We must also recognize that human life is impermanent. Death will come, and it can occur at any moment. Buddhists believe that the way they have conducted their lives will determine how they live in the next life. That is the reason it is important to practice the dharma, the teachings of the Buddha. This helps each person face death without fear, knowing that he or she will be reborn into a happier life.

THE AWAKENING MIND

According to the Dalai Lama, the awakening mind is the way to eventually achieve nirvana. Achieving an awakening mind

begins by developing compassion for all other human beings—
our enemies as well as people we may not even know. This may
seem difficult, but the Dalai Lama urges us to realize that in a
former life, an enemy may have been a relative whom we loved
very dearly. Someone we don't know may have been a close
friend. Considering these possibilities makes it easier to feel
compassion for these people and have patience with them, while
avoiding anger or jealousy.

If we recognize that others are just like ourselves, it is also
easier to feel compassion for them. Other people want to
enjoy life and avoid suffering, just as we do. Knowing this
helps us focus less on our own needs and wants and more on
the needs of others. Instead of blaming others for actions
that make us feel bad, we should look inside ourselves. We
must begin to discipline our minds and change them
through prayer and meditation. This enables us to replace
anger with understanding, and criticism with patience.
Indeed, we might thank others who try our patience for
teaching us to develop more of it. This will train us to feel
compassion for others. Only through compassion can we
achieve a happy rebirth in the next life and eventually reach
nirvana. As the Buddha stated: "I have shown you the path of
liberation [nirvana]. However, you should know that your
liberation depends on you." [50]

The Dalai Lama has advocated a middle way that lies
between our own needs and the needs of others. But if we
must choose, then other people's needs must come first. He
encourages us to meditate on giving away what we own for
the benefit of others. This includes giving others our material
possessions as well as sharing our qualities of love and understanding. We should also meditate on taking away the sufferings
of others. Then we should put our meditations into practice
in the world. This is the essence of the awakening mind.
However, achieving a fully awakened mind and reaching
nirvana may take several lifetimes to accomplish. We must live
and be reborn over and over again.

ETHICS FOR THE TWENTY-FIRST CENTURY

From his home in Dharamsala, the Dalai Lama meets with people of many religions who deal with suffering in their lives. As he wrote in his book *Ethics for the New Millennium,* all of them are looking for the answer to the same question: "How am I to be happy?" [51] As the Dalai Lama has pointed out, many people seem to think that money, cars, and beautiful homes will satisfy their needs. Yet even after they acquire these things they suffer from anxiety, stress, and general unhappiness.

Instead of material wealth, the Dalai Lama has emphasized spiritual values. The basis of these values is the desire to help others and look out for their interests. As he said, these values reflect the Tibetan saying, *shen pen kyi sem,* "the thought to be of help to others." [52] These spiritual values should form the basis of

DHARAMSALA

Today, the Tibetan government in exile has its headquarters at Dharamsala in northern India. Here, Tibetans display Buddhist prayer flags from their homes. Tibetan exiles attend religious celebrations at Buddhist temples. They prostrate themselves before Buddhist images and make offerings to statues of the Buddha. Over the decades since the Dalai Lama fled to India, more than ten monasteries have been established in Dharamsala. These are run by Buddhist monks and nuns. The monasteries are centers of Buddhist learning. They also have schools where children who have escaped from Tibet or grown up in India can receive an education. In addition to these schools, the Dalai Lama has established the Tibetan archives at Dharamsala. These hold many books and manuscripts that are sacred to Buddhism.

From exile in Dharamsala, the Dalai Lama recognized a six-year-old boy whom he regarded as the reincarnation of the Panchen Lama. However, this boy was arrested by the Chinese and has been held by them since the mid-1990s. Fearing for his safety, Ogyen Trinley Dorje, who is the third most important leader of Tibetan Buddhism, escaped from Tibet late in 1999 and sought refuge in Dharamsala. Ogyen Trinley Dorje is the *karmapa,* the spiritual head of the Karma Kagyu tradition of Tibetan Buddhism. Upon his escape, he decided to continue his religious studies in India.

our ethical approach to life. That is, our ethics should involve avoiding any actions that harm others and only doing good in our relationships with people. Right is being good to others and helping them achieve happiness, while wrong is being harmful and bringing other people unhappiness.

Human beings are, by nature, social creatures. The Dalai Lama has emphasized that we are unable to "bear the sight of another's suffering." We have the ability to empathize with others. That is, we can put ourselves in their shoes and understand how they feel. We also rely on the kindness of others. It is very difficult for us to accomplish anything by ourselves. For example, we rely on our family to provide us with shelter, food, and love. This process begins when we are helpless infants, completely dependent upon our parents. Similarly, we rely on our friends to give us understanding, to share experiences, and to help us with our work in school or on a job. According to the Dalai Lama:

> Basic human nature is not only non-violent but actually disposed toward love and compassion, kindness, gentleness, affection creation, and so on. . . . It follows, therefore, that if we could enhance the capacity—that is to say, our sensitivity toward others' suffering—the more we did so, the less we could tolerate seeing others' pain and the more we would be concerned to ensure that no action of ours caused harm to others.[53]

This increases our sense of what is right and our desire to avoid what is wrong.

However, the Dalai Lama recognizes that there are selfish people in the world who seem to think only of themselves. Some of them may seem to be very successful, since they may possess money and power. They often feel alone, however. Any friends they have are most likely only interested in their money or power. Once the selfish person loses these things, he or she no longer has any friends, and has no way to receive any support, compassion, or understanding.

LEADING A VIRTUOUS LIFE

The Dalai Lama has emphasized that the key to leading an ethical life is to restrain negative feelings—such as anger, hatred, and jealously—and to practice positive ones. In Tibet, the term *so pa* means "courage when life does not turn out as we want it." By practicing so pa, Buddhists are able to limit their negative emotions and hold back their anger, even when someone treats them unfairly. The Dalai Lama has also stated that there may be times when it is appropriate to express anger. But by practicing so pa, we reserve our anger for use only when someone has done something that is inexcusably hurtful—for example, using violence against another person. At other times, we practice patience and accept life as it comes, even though it will not always satisfy us.

An ethical life, according to the Dalai Lama, depends on practicing virtues such as compassion, fortitude, and forgiveness. Another important virtue is humility. Practicing humility enables us to restrain a negative emotion—pride. Humility does not mean a lack of self-confidence. An individual can be confident in his or her ability to make decisions, for example, without bragging about it or being conceited. Individuals with pride and conceit are self-centered. This prevents them from showing compassion for others.

The Dalai Lama is fully aware that practicing these virtues is not easy:

> Making a habit of concern for others' well-being, and spending a few minutes on waking in the morning reflecting on the value of conducting our lives in an ethically disciplined manner, is a good way to start the day. . . . The same is true of taking some time at the end of each day to review how successful in this we have been.[54]

The goal, according to the Dalai Lama, is what the Tibetans call *nying je chenmo,* or "great compassion." This is a great sensitivity to any suffering experienced by other people anywhere in the world and a desire to do everything possible to eliminate this suffering. Finally, it enables us to take on what the Dalai Lama has called "universal responsibility." This means looking beyond our family and friends to the needs of people we may not even know. Instead of allowing ourselves to be divided by differences of religion, skin color, or nationality, we must recognize all the attributes that humans share. As a result, each of us should work to make sure that others receive the care, justice, and happiness they deserve.

DALAI LAMA

The ancient religion of Buddhism takes its name not from a primary deity, as Christianity does, but from the title bestowed upon its founder—Siddhartha Gautama, known as the Buddha. The Buddha is depicted in religious artwork, like this painting housed in the Tibetan Museum, as an idealized figure. He represents the epitome of the enlightened soul all Buddhists wish to become.

One of the most recognizable symbols of the Buddhist religion is the mandala, or wheel of life, which represents the many facets of both the physical and spiritual worlds that have an effect on a person as he or she searches for enlightenment. This colorful illustration is a Tibetan version of the mandala, known as a Tibetan Mandala Thanka.

After the death of the Thirteenth Dalai Lama in 1933, a search began for the child who would be the reincarnation of the great leader. That child turned out to be Lhamo Dhondup (later Tenzin Gyatso, the Fourteenth Dalai Lama), who was born on July 6, 1935, in the village of Taktser in rural northeastern Tibet. This undated photograph was likely taken of the future spiritual leader soon before his installation as Dalai Lama in February 1940.

Prior to his flight from Tibet, the Dalai Lama had his official residence here, at Potala Palace, the magnificent structure located at the summit of the Marpori (or red mountain) in Tibet.

During the Chinese invasion of Tibet in 1950, there was great confusion among the Dalai Lama's advisors as to what should be done with the Tibetan government and its young leader. Tenzin Gyatso was only a teenager at the time, but he was nonetheless made the official head of the Tibetan state as the nation tried to negotiate with the invaders. This photograph of the Fourteenth Dalai Lama was taken on November 7, 1950, while he was being detained by the heads of the Tibetan Buddhist monasteries who were opposed to his intention to leave Tibet.

On a trip to India during a goodwill tour celebrating the twenty-five-hundredth anniversary of the birth of the Buddha, the Dalai Lama became acquainted with Indian Prime Minister Jawaharlal Nehru. The two men are seen here riding an elephant together in November 1956. The Dalai Lama is at center and Nehru is at rear.

Still in exile after almost half a century, the Fourteenth Dalai Lama works hard to make the international public aware of the plight of Tibet and the continuing traditions of Tibetan Buddhism. These Buddhist monks are lighting oil lamps during a January 13, 2003, festival called "Kalchakra." This ten-day celebration was started by the Dalai Lama in Bodhgaya, in Bihar state, the town where the Buddha achieved enlightenment.

Despite his lengthy exile and the many political crises he has faced, the Dalai Lama always maintains a positive outlook, trusting in his Buddhist faith to help him achieve his goals. He is seen here praying at the Ananda Budhha Vihara Temple in Hyderabad, India, in April 2003, during ceremonies to inaugurate the new temple, which was built on Mahindra Hill in the southern Indian state of Andhra Pradesh.

Roles of the Dalai Lama

*I pray for all of us, oppressor and friend, that together
we succeed in building a better world through human
understanding and love, and that in doing so we may
reduce the pain and suffering of all sentient beings. . . .
I am optimistic that the ancient values that have
sustained mankind are today reaffirming themselves to
prepare us for a kinder, happier twenty-first century.*

— Tenzin Gyatso, the Fourteenth Dalai Lama

The current Dalai Lama is the heir to several rich traditions. One of these is Buddhism, founded twenty-five hundred years ago by the Buddha, Siddhartha Gautama. It is one of the world's oldest religions. Another tradition is the particular form of Buddhism practiced in Tibet, introduced to the country during the seventh century. Finally, he is the heir to the thirteen Dalai Lamas who preceded him; a lineage that began during the fourteenth century.

Today, the Dalai Lama is one of the world's most prominent leaders. Like his predecessors, he is the spiritual leader of Tibetan Buddhists. Many of these people remain in Tibet, even though the nation has been under the control of the Chinese Communists since 1950. Buddhists continue to practice their beliefs, despite the fact that they are discouraged—at times violently—from doing so by the Communist-controlled government. Some Buddhists have even paid with their lives for their religious beliefs at the hands of the Chinese. Other Tibetan Buddhists have escaped from their country. Today, they live in India, Nepal, and other nations, where they continue to practice their unique version of Buddhism.

In addition to being the spiritual leader of Tibetan Buddhism, the Fourteenth Dalai Lama is the political leader of Tibet. Since 1959, he has maintained a government in exile in India. From his headquarters in Dharamsala, he has publicized to the world the plight of the Tibetans under Chinese Communist rule. This has given him a role unlike that played by any of his predecessors. The Dalai Lama has traveled widely and spoken to many foreign government leaders about the political situation in Tibet in hopes of winning support for his country. Although no nation formally recognizes his government in exile, the Dalai Lama has not given up on his efforts to bring the world's attention to the current conditions inside Tibet.

Finally, the Fourteenth Dalai Lama has become an international spiritual leader. Through his many books, teachings, and speeches, he has brought Buddhism to the attention of a worldwide audience. More people than ever before—especially in the United States and Europe—have become aware of the principles of Buddhism. Many have even embraced the Buddhist religion.

Wherever he travels, the Dalai Lama brings his simple message of love and compassion to the people who come to hear him speak. As the Dalai Lama himself has put it:

> I am convinced that despite different cultures and different political and economic systems, we are all basically the same. The more people I meet the stronger my conviction becomes that the oneness of humanity, founded on understanding and respect, is a realistic and viable basis for our conduct. Wherever I go, this is what I speak about. I believe that the practice of compassion and love—a genuine sense of brotherhood and sisterhood—is the universal religion.[55]

APPENDIX

THE SEVENTEEN POINT AGREEMENT (1951)

ONE—The Tibetan people shall unite and drive out imperialist aggressive forces from Tibet; the Tibetan people shall return to the family of the motherland—the People's Republic of China.

TWO—The Local Government of Tibet shall actively assist the People's Liberation Army to enter Tibet and consolidate the national defence.

THREE—In accordance with the policy towards nationalities laid down in the *Common Programme of the Chinese Political Consultative Conference,* the Tibetan people have the right to exercise national regional autonomy under the unified leadership of the Central People's Government.

FOUR—The central authorities will not alter the existing political system in Tibet. The central authorities also will not alter the established status, functions, and powers of the Dalai Lama. Officials of various rank shall hold office as usual.

FIVE—The established status, functions and powers of the Bainqen Erdini shall be maintained.

SIX—By the established status, functions, and powers of the Dalai Lama and of the Bainqen Erdini are meant the status, functions and powers of the 13th Dalai Lama and the 9th Bainqen when they were in friendly and amicable relation with each other.

SEVEN—The policy of freedom of religious belief laid down in the *Common Programme of the Chinese Political Consultative Conference* shall be carried out. The religious beliefs, customs and habits of the Tibetan people shall be respected, and lama monasteries shall be protected. The central authorities will not effect a change in the income of the monasteries.

EIGHT—Tibetan troops shall be reorganized by stages into the People's Liberation Army, and become a part of the national defence forces of the People's Republic of China.

NINE—The spoken and written language and school education of the Tibetan nationality shall be developed step by step in accordance with the actual conditions in Tibet.

TEN—Tibetan agriculture, livestock raising, industry and commerce shall be dveloped step by step, and the people's livelihood shall be improved step by step in accordance with the actual conditions in Tibet.

ELEVEN—In matters related to various reforms in Tibet there will be no compulsion on the part of the central authorities. The Local Government of Tibet should carry out reforms of its own accord, and demands for reform raised by the people shall be settled by means of consultation with the lading personnel of Tibet.

TWELVE—In so far as former pro-imperialist and pro-Kuomintang officials resolutely sever relations with imperialism and the Kuomintang, and do not engage in sabotage or resistance, they may continue to hold office irrespective of their past.

THIRTEEN—The People's Liberation Army entering Tibet shall abide by all the above mentioned policies and sahll also be fair in all buying and selling and shall not arbitrarily take a single needle or thread from the people.

FOURTEEN—The Central People's Government shall conduct the centralized handling of all external affairs of Tibet and there will be peaceful coexistence with neighbouring countries and the establishment and development of fair commercial and trading relations with them on the basis of equality, mutual benefit and mutual respect for territory and sovereignty.

FIFTEEN—In order to ensure the implementation of this agreement, the Central People's Government shall set up a military and administrative committee and a military area headquarters in Tibet, and apart from the personnel sent there by the Central People's Government, shall absorb as many local Tibetan personnel as possible to take part in the work. Local

APPENDIX

Tibetan personnel taking part in the military and administrative committee may include patriotic elements from the Local Government of Tibet, various districts and leading monasteries; the name-list shall be drawn up after consultation between the representative designated by the Central People's Government and the various quarters concerned, and shall be submitted to the Central People's Government for appointment.

SIXTEEN—Funds needed by the military and administrative committee, the military area headquarters and the People's Liberation Army entering Tibet shall be provided by the Central People's Government. The Local Government of Tibet will assist the People's Liberation Army in the purchase and transport of food,fodder, and other daily necessities.

SEVENTEEN—This agreement sahll come into force immediately after signatures and seals are affixed to it.

Signed in Beijing on the 23rd of May 1951

Chinese Representatives:
Li Weihan, Zhang Jingwu, Zhang Guohua and Sun Zhiyuan

Tibetan Representatives:
Ngabo Ngawang Jigme, Khame Sonam Wangdu, Lhawutara Thupten Tenther, Thupten Lekmon and Sampho Tenzin Dhundup

THE DALAI LAMA'S FIVE-POINT PEACE PLAN

Address to Members of the United States Congress. The Five Point Peace Plan for Tibet, by His Holiness the Dalai Lama, Washington, D.C., September 21, 1987.

INTRODUCTION

The world is increasingly interdependent, so that lasting peace—national, regional, and global—can only be achieved if we think in terms of broader interest rather than parochial needs. At this time, it is crucial that all of us, the strong and the weak, contribute in our own way. I speak to you today as the leader of the Tibetan people and as a Buddhist monk devoted to the principles of a religion based on love and compassion. Above all, I am here as a human being who is destined to share this planet with you and all others as brothers and sisters. As the world grows smaller, we need each other more than in the past. This is true in all parts of the world, including the continent I come from. At present in Asia, as elsewhere, tensions are high. There are open conflicts in the Middle East, Southeast Asia, and in my own country, Tibet. To a large extent, these problems are symptoms of the underlying tensions that exist among the area's great powers. In order to resolve regional conflicts, an approach is required that takes into account the interests of all relevant countries and peoples, large and small. Unless comprehensive solutions are formulated, that take into account the aspirations of the people most directly concerned, piecemeal or merely expedient measures will only create new problems.

The Tibetan people are eager to contribute to regional and world peace, and I believe they are in a unique position to do so. Traditionally, Tibetans are a peace loving and non-violent people. Since Buddhism was introduced to Tibet over one thousand years ago, Tibetans have practiced non-violence with respect to all forms of life. This attitude has also been extended to our country's international relations. Tibet's highly strategic position in the heart of Asia, separating the continent's great powers—India, China and the USSR—has throughout history endowed it with an essential role in the maintenance of peace and stability. This is precisely why, in the past, Asia's empires went to great lengths to keep one another out of Tibet. Tibet's value as an independent buffer state was integral to the region's stability. When the newly formed People's Republic of China invaded Tibet in 1949/50, it created a new source of conflict. This was highlighted when, following the Tibetan national uprising against the Chinese and my flight to India in 1959, tensions between China and India escalated into the border war in 1962. Today large numbers of troops are again massed on both sides of the Himalayan border and tension is once more dangerously high.

The real issue, of course, is not the Indo-Tibetan border demarcation. It is China's illegal occupation of Tibet, which has given it direct access to the Indian sub-continent. The Chinese authorities have attempted to confuse the issue by claiming that Tibet has always been a part of China. This is untrue. Tibet was a fully independent state when the People's Liberation Army invaded the country in 1949/50.

Since Tibetan emperors unified Tibet, over a thousand years ago, our country was able to maintain its independence until the middle of this century. At times Tibet extended its influence over neighbouring countries and peoples and, in other periods, came itself under the influence of powerful foreign rulers—the Mongol Khans, the Gorkhas of Nepal, the Manchu Emperors and the British in India.

It is, of course, not uncommon for states to be subjected to foreign influence or interference. Although so-called satellite relationships are perhaps the clearest example of this, most major powers exert influence over less powerful allies or neighbours. As the most authoritative legal studies have shown, in Tibet's case, the country's occasional subjection to foreign influence never entailed a loss of independence. And there can be no doubt that when Peking's communist armies entered Tibet, Tibet was in all respects an independent state.

China's aggression, condemned by virtually all nations of the free world, was a flagrant violation of international law. As China's military occupation of Tibet continues, the world should remember that though Tibetans have lost their freedom, under international law Tibet today is still an independent state under illegal occupation.

It is not my purpose to enter a political/legal discussion here concerning Tibet's status. I just wish to emphasise the obvious and undisputed fact that we Tibetans are a distinct people with our own culture, language, religion and history. But for China's occupation, Tibet would still, today, fulfil its natural role as a buffer state maintaining and promoting peace in Asia.

It is my sincere desire, as well as that of the Tibetan people, to restore to Tibet her invaluable role, by converting the entire country—comprising the three provinces of U-Tsang, Kham and Amdo—once more into a place of stability, peace and harmony. In the best of Buddhist tradition, Tibet would extend its services and hospitality to all who further the cause of world peace and the well-being of mankind and the natural environment we share.

Despite the holocaust inflicted upon our people in the past decades of occupation, I have always strived to find a solution through direct and honest discussions with the Chinese. In 1982, following the change of leadership in China and the establishment of direct contacts with the government in Peking, I sent my representatives to Peking to open talks concerning the future of my country and people.

We entered the dialogue with a sincere and positive attitude and with a willingness to take into account the legitimate needs of the People's Republic of China. I had hoped that this attitude would be reciprocated and that a solution could eventually be found which would satisfy and safeguard the aspirations and interests of both parties. Unfortunately, China has consistently responded to our efforts in a defensive manner, as though our detailing of Tibet's very real difficulties was criticism for its own sake.

To our even greater dismay, the Chinese government misused the opportunity for a genuine dialogue. Instead of addressing the real issues facing the six million Tibetan people, China has attempted to reduce the question of Tibet to a discussion of my own personal status.

It is against this background and in response to the tremendous support and encouragement I have been given by you and other persons I have met during this trip, that I wish today to clarify the principal issues and to propose, in a spirit of openness and conciliation, a first step towards a lasting solution. I hope this may contribute to a future of friendship and cooperation with all of our neighbours, including the Chinese people.

This peace plan contains five basic components:

1. Transformation of the whole of Tibet into a zone of peace;

2. Abandonment of China's population transfer policy which threatens the very existence of the Tibetans as a people;

3.   Respect for the Tibetan people's fundamental human rights and democratic freedoms;

4.   Restoration and protection of Tibet's natural environment and the abandonment of China's use of Tibet for the production of nuclear weapons and dumping of nuclear waste;

5.   Commencement of earnest negotiations on the future status of Tibet and of relations between the Tibetan and Chinese people.

Let me explain these five components:

1.   I propose that the whole of Tibet, including the eastern provinces of Kham and Amdo, be transformed into a zone of "ahimsa," a Hindi term used to mean a state of peace and non-violence.

The establishment of such a peace zone would be in keeping with Tibet's historical role as a peaceful and neutral Buddhist nation and buffer state separating the continent's great powers. It would also be in keeping with Nepal's proposal to proclaim Nepal a peace zone and with China's declared support for such a proclamation. The peace zone proposed by Nepal would have a much greater impact if it were to include Tibet and neighbouring areas.

The establishing of a peace zone on Tibet would require withdrawal of Chinese troops and military installations from the country, which would enable India also to withdraw troops and military installations from the Himalayan regions bordering Tibet. This would be achieved under an international agreement which would satisfy China's legitimate security needs and build trust among the Tibetan, Indian, Chinese and other peoples of the region. This is in everyone's best interest, particularly that of China and India, as it would enhance their security, while reducing the economic burden of maintaining high troop concentrations on the disputed Himalayan border.

Historically, relations between China and India were never strained. It was only when Chinese armies marched into Tibet, creating for the first time a common border, that tensions arose between these two powers, ultimately leading to the 1962 war. Since then numerous dangerous incidents have continued to occur. A restoration of good relations between the world's two most populous countries would be greatly facilitated if they were separated—as they were throughout history—by a large and friendly buffer region.

To improve relations between the Tibetan People and the Chinese, the first requirement is the creation of trust. After the holocaust of the last decades in which over one million Tibetans—one sixth of the population—lost their lives and at least as many lingered in prison camps because of their religious beliefs and love of freedom, only a withdrawal of Chinese troops could start a genuine process of reconciliation. The vast occupation force in Tibet is a daily reminder to the Tibetans of the oppression and suffering they have all experienced. A troop withdrawal would be an essential signal that in the future a meaningful relationship might be established with the Chinese, based on friendship and trust.

2.   The population transfer of Chinese into Tibet, which the government in Peking pursues in order to force a "final solution" to the Tibetan problem by reducing the Tibetan population to an insignificant and disenfranchised minority in Tibet itself, must be stopped.

The massive transfer of Chinese civilians into Tibet in violation of the Fourth Geneva Convention (1949), threatens the very existence of the Tibetans as a distinct people. In the eastern parts of our country, the Chinese now greatly outnumber Tibetans. In the Amdo province, for example, where I was born, there are, according to Chinese statistics, 2.5 million Chinese and only 750,000 Tibetans. Even in the so-called Tibet Autonomous Region (i.e.: central and western Tibet), Chinese government sources now confirm that Chinese outnumber Tibetans.

The Chinese population transfer policy is not new. It has been systematically applied to other areas before. Earlier in this century, the Manchus were a distinct race with their own culture and traditions. Today only two to three million Manchurians are left in Manchuria, where 75 million Chinese have settled. In Eastern

Turkestan, which the Chinese now call Sinkiang [Xinjiang], the Chinese population has grown from 200,000 in 1949 to seven million,more than half of the total population of 13 million. In the wake of the Chinese colonisation of Inner Mongolia, Chinese number 8.5 million, Mongols 2.5 million.

Today, in the whole of Tibet 7.5 million Chinese settlers have already been sent, outnumbering the Tibetan population of six million. In central and western Tibet, now referred to by the Chinese as the "Tibetan Autonomous Region," Chinese sources admit the 1.9 million Tibetans already constitute a minority of the region's population. These numbers do not take the estimated 300,000–500,000 troops in Tibet into account—250,000 of them in the so-called Tibetan Autonomous Region.

For the Tibetans to survive as a people, it is imperative that the population transfer is stopped and the Chinese settlers return to China. Otherwise, Tibetans will soon be no more than a tourist attraction and relic of a noble past.

3. Fundamental human rights and democratic freedoms must be respected in Tibet. The Tibetan people must once again be free to develop culturally, intellectually, economically and spiritually and to exercise basic democratic freedoms.

    Human rights violations in Tibet are among the most serious in the world. Discrimination is practiced in Tibet under a policy of "apartheid" which the Chinese call "segregation and assimilation." Tibetans are, at best, second class citizens in their own country. Deprived of all basic democratic rights and freedoms, they exist under a colonial administration in which all real power is wielded by Chinese officials of the Communist Party and the army.

    Although the Chinese government allows Tibetans to rebuild some Buddhist monasteries and to worship in them, it still forbids serious study and teaching of religion. Only a small number of people, approved by the Communist party, are allowed to join the monasteries.

    While Tibetans in exile exercise their democratic rights under a constitution promulgated by me in 1963, thousands of our countrymen suffer in prisons and labour camps in Tibet for their religious or political convictions.

4. Serious efforts must be made to restore the natural environment in Tibet. Tibet should not be used for the production of nuclear weapons and the dumping of nuclear waste.

    Tibetans have a great respect for all forms of life. This inherent feeling is enhanced by the Buddhist faith, which prohibits the harming of all sentient beings, whether human or animal. Prior to the Chinese invasion, Tibet was an unspoiled wilderness sanctuary in a unique natural environment. Sadly, in the past decades the wildlife and the forests of Tibet have been almost totally destroyed by the Chinese. The effects on Tibet's delicate environment have been devastating. What little is left in Tibet must be protected and efforts must be made to restore the environment to its balanced state.

    China uses Tibet for the production of nuclear weapons and may also have started dumping nuclear waste in Tibet. Not only does China plan to dispose of its own nuclear waste but also that of other countries, who have already agreed to pay Peking to dispose of their toxic materials.

    The dangers this presents are obvious. Not only living generations, but future generations are threatened by China's lack of concern for Tibet's unique and delicate environment.

5. Negotiations on the future status of Tibet and the relationship between the Tibetan and Chinese peoples should be started in earnest.

    We wish to approach this subject in a reasonable and realistic way, in a spirit of frankness and conciliation and with a view to finding a solution that is in the long term interest of all: the Tibetans, the Chinese, and all other peoples concerned. Tibetans and Chinese are distinct people, each with their own country, history, culture, language and way of life. Differences among peoples must be recognised and respected. They need not, however, form obstacles to genuine cooperation where this is in the mutual benefit of both peoples. It is my sincere belief that if the concerned parties were to meet and discuss their future with an open mind and a sincere desire to find a satisfactory and just solution, a breakthrough could be achieved. We must all exert ourselves to be reasonable and wise, and to meet in a spirit of frankness and understanding.

Let me end on a personal note. I wish to thank you for your concern and support which you and so many of your colleagues and fellow citizens have expressed for the plight of oppressed people everywhere. The fact that you have publicly shown your sympathy for us Tibetans has already had a positive impact on the lives of our people inside Tibet. I ask for your continued support in this critical time in our country's history.

Thank you.

U.S. CONGRESS FOREIGN RELATIONS AUTHORIZATION ACT FOR FISCAL YEAR 1988–1989 (EXCERPT)

DECEMBER 22, 1987

SEC 1243. HUMAN RIGHTS VIOLATIONS IN TIBET BY THE PEOPLE'S REPUBLIC OF CHINA

(A) Findings—The Congress finds that:

(1) on October 1, 1987, Chinese police in Lhasa fired upon several thousand unarmed Tibetan demonstrators, which included hundreds of women, children, and Tibetan Buddhist monks, killing at least six and wounding many others;

(2) on September 27, 1987, a peaceful demonstration in Lhasa calling for Tibetan independence and the restoration of human rights in Tibet, which was led by hundreds of Tibetan monks, was violently broken up by Chinese authorities and 27 Tibetan Buddhist monks were arrested;

(3) in the wake of His Holiness the Dalai Lama's five point peace plan, which was presented to Members of the United States Congress during his visit to Washington in September 1987, Chinese authorities in Tibet staged, on September 24, 1987, a mass political rally at which three Tibetans were given death sentences, two of whom were executed immediately;

(4) beginning October 7, 1950, the Chinese Communist army invaded and occupied Tibet;

(5) since that time, the Chinese Government has exercised dominion over the Tibetan people, who had always considered themselves as independent, through the presence of a large occupation force;

(6) over 1,000,000 Tibetans perished from 1959 to 1979 as a direct result of the political instability, executions, imprisonment, and wide scale famine engendered by the policies of the People's Republic of China in Tibet;

(7) after 1950, particularly during the ravages of China's Cultural Revolution, over 6,000 monasteries, the repositories of 1,300 years of Tibet's ancient civilization, were destroyed and their irreplaceable national legacy of art and literature either destroyed, stolen, or removed from Tibet;

(8) the exploitation of Tibet's vast mineral, forest, and animal reserves has occurred with limited benefit to the Tibetan people;

(9) Tibet's economy and education, health, and human services remain far below those of the People's Republic of China as a whole;

(10) the People's Republic of China has encouraged a large influx of Han-Chinese into Tibet, thereby undermining the political and cultural traditions of the Tibetan people;

(11) there are credible reports of many Tibetans being incarcerated in labor camps and prisons and killed for the nonviolent expression of their religious and political beliefs;

(12) His Holiness the Dalai Lama, spiritual and temporal leader of the Tibetan people, in conjunction with the 100,000 refugees forced into exile with him, has worked tirelessly for almost 30 years to secure peace and religious freedom in Tibet, as well as the preservation of the Tibetan culture;

(13) in 1959, 1961, and 1965, the United Nations General Assembly called upon the People's Republic of China to end the violations of Tibetans' human rights;

(14) on July 24, 1985, 91 Members of the Congress signed a letter to President Li Xiannian of the People's Republic of China expressing support for direct talks between Beijing and representatives of His Holiness the Dalai Lama and the Tibetans in exile, and urging the Government of the People's Republic of China "to grant the very reasonable and justified aspirations of His Holiness the Dalai Lama and his people every consideration;"

(15) on September 27, 1987, the chairman and ranking minority member of the Senate Foreign Relations Committee, the chairman and ranking minority member of the House Foreign Affairs Committee, and the Co-chairman of the Congressional Human Rights Caucus signed a letter to his Excellency Zhao Ziyang, the Prime Minister of the People's Republic of China, expressing their "grave concern with the present situation in Tibet and welcome(d) His Holiness the Dalai Lama's (five point) peace proposal as a historic step toward resolving the important question of Tibet and alleviating the suffering of the Tibetan people . . . (and expressing) their full support for his proposal;" and

(16) there has been no positive response by the Government of the People's Republic of China to either of these communications.

(B) STATEMENT OF POLICIES—It is the sense of the Congress that:

(1) the United States should express sympathy for those Tibetans who have suffered and died as a result of fighting, persecution, or famine over the past four decades;

(2) the United States should make the treatment of the Tibetan people an important factor in its conduct of relations with the People's Republic of China;

(3) the Government of the People's Republic of China should respect internationally recognized human rights and end human rights violations against Tibetans;

(4) the United States should urge the Government of the People's Republic of China to actively reciprocate the Dalai Lama's efforts to establish a constructive dialogue on the future of Tibet;

(5) Tibetan culture and religion should be preserved and the Dalai Lama should be commended for his efforts in this regard;

(6) the United States, through the Secretary of State, should address and call attention to the rights of the Tibetan people, as well as other non-Han-Chinese within the People's Republic of China such as the Uighurs of Eastern Turkestan (Xinjiang), and the Mongolians of Inner Mongolia;

(7) the President should instruct United States officials, including the United States Ambassadors to the People's Republic of China and India, to pay greater attention to the concerns of the Tibetan people and to work closely with all concerned about human rights violations in Tibet in order to find areas in which the United States Government and people can be helpful; and

(8) the United States should urge the People's Republic of China to release all political prisoners in Tibet.

(C) TRANSFER OF DEFENSE ARTICLES—With respect to any sale, licensed export, or other transfer of any defense articles or defense services to the People's Republic of China, the United States Government shall, consistent with United States law, take into account the extent to which the Government of the People's Republic of China is acting in good faith and in a timely manner to resolve human rights issues in Tibet.

(D) MIGRATION AND REFUGEE ASSISTANCE—Within 60 days after the date of the enactment of this Act, the Secretary of State shall determine whether the needs of displaced Tibetans are similar to those of displaced persons and refugees in other parts of the world and shall report that determination to the Congress. If the Secretary makes a positive determination, of the amounts authorized to be appropriated for the Department of State for "Migration and Refugee Assistance" for each of the fiscal years 1988 and 1989, such sums as are necessary shall be made available for assistance for displaced Tibetans. The Secretary of State shall determine the best means for providing such assistance.

(E) SCHOLARSHIPS—For each of the fiscal years 1988 and 1989, the Director of the United States Information Agency shall make available to Tibetan students and professionals who are outside Tibet no less than 15 scholarships for study at institutions of higher education in the United States.

APPENDIX

THE NOBEL LECTURE

On December 11, 1989, the day after receiving the Nobel Peace Prize, His Holiness the Dalai Lama delivered this lecture at Osloís University Aula.

Brothers and Sisters, it is an honor and pleasure to be among you today. I am really happy to see so many old friends who have come from different corners of the world, and to make new friends, whom I hope to meet again in the future. When I meet people in different parts of the world, I am always reminded that we are all basically alike: we are all human beings. Maybe we have different clothes, our skin is of a different color, or we speak different languages. That is on the surface. But basically, we are the same human beings. That is what binds us to each other. That is what makes it possible for us to understand each other and to develop friendship and closeness.

Thinking over what I might say today, I decided to share with you some of my thoughts concerning the common problems all of us face as members of the human family. Because we all share this small planet earth, we have to learn to live in harmony and peace with each other and with nature. That is not just a dream, but a necessity. We are dependent on each other in so many ways that we can no longer live in isolated communities and ignore what is happening outside those communities. We need to help each other when we have difficulties, and we must share the good fortune that we enjoy. I speak to you as just another human being; as a simple monk. If you find what I say useful, then I hope you will try to practice it.

I also wish to share with you today my feelings concerning the plight and aspirations of the people of Tibet. The Nobel Prize is a prize they well deserve for their courage and unfailing determination during the last forty years of foreign occupation. As a free spokesman for my captive countrymen and women, I feel it is my duty to speak out on their behalf. I speak without a feeling of anger or hatred towards those who are responsible for the immense suffering of our people and the destruction of our land, home and culture. They too are human beings who struggle to find happiness and deserve our compassion. I speak to inform you of the sad situation in my country today and of the aspirations of my people, because in our struggle for freedom, truth is the only weapon we possess.

The realization that we are all basically the same human beings, who seek happiness and try to avoid suffering is very helpful in developing a sense of brotherhood and sisterhood; a warm feeling of love and compassion for others. This, in turn, is essential if we are to survive in the ever-shrinking world we live in. For if we each selfishly pursue only what we believe to be in our own interest, without caring about the needs of others, we not only may end up harming others but also ourselves. This fact has become very clear during the course of this century. We know that to wage a nuclear war today, for example, would be a form of suicide; or that by polluting the air or the oceans, in order to achieve some short-term benefit, we are destroying the very basis for our survival. As individuals and nations becoming increasingly inter-dependent, therefore, we have no other choice than to develop what I call a sense of universal responsibility.

Today, we are truly a global family. What happens in one part of the world may affect us all. This, of course, is not only true of the negative things that happen, but is equally valid for the positive developments. We not only know what happens elsewhere, thanks to the extraordinary modern communications technology, we are also directly affected by events that occur far away. We feel a sense of sadness when children are starving in Eastern Africa. Similarly, we feel a sense of joy when a family is reunited after decades of separation by the Berlin Wall. Our crops and livestock are contaminated and our health and livelihood threatened when a nuclear accident happens miles away in another country. Our own security is enhanced when peace breaks out between warring parties in other continents.

But war or peace; the destruction or the protection of nature; the violation or promotion of human rights and democratic freedoms; poverty or material well-being; the lack of moral and spiritual values or their existence and development; and the breakdown or develop-ment of human understanding, are not isolated phenomena that can be analyzed and tackled independently of one another. In fact, they are very much interrelated at all levels and need to be approached with that understanding.

Peace, in the sense of the absence of war, is of little value to someone who is dying of hunger or cold. It will not remove the pain of torture inflicted on a prisoner of conscience. It does not comfort those who have lost their loved ones in floods caused by senseless deforestation in a neighboring country. Peace can only last where human rights are respected, where the people are fed, and where individuals and nations are free. True peace with oneself and with the world around us can only be achieved through the development of mental peace. The other phenomena mentioned above are similarly interrelated. Thus, for example, we see that a clean environment, wealth or democracy mean little in the face of war, especially nuclear war, and that material development is not sufficient to ensure human happiness.

Material progress is of course important for human advancement. In Tibet, we paid much to little attention to technological and economic development, and today we realize that this was a mistake. At the same time, material development without spiritual development can also cause serious problems. In some countries too much attention is paid to external things and very little importance is given to inner development. I believe both are important and must be developed side by side so as to achieve a good balance between them. Tibetans are always described by foreign visitors as being a happy, jovial people. This is part of our national character, formed by cultural and religious values that stress the importance of mental peace through the generation of love and kindness to all other living sentient beings, both human and animal. Inner peace is the key: if you have inner peace, the external problems do not affect your deep sense of peace and tranquillity. In that state of mind you can deal with situations with calmness and reason, while keeping your inner happiness. This is very important. Without this inner peace, no matter how comfortable your life is materially, you may still be worried, disturbed or unhappy because of circumstances.

Clearly, it is of great importance, therefore, to understand the interrelationship among these and other phenomena to approach and attempt to solve problems in a balanced way that takes these different aspects into consideration. Of course it is not easy. But it is of little benefit to try to solve one problem if doing so creates an equally serious new one. So really we have no alternative: we must develop a sense of universal responsibility not only in the geographic sense, but also in respect to the different issues that confront our planet.

Responsibility does not only lie with the leaders of our countries or with those who have been appointed or elected to do a particular job. It lies with each of us individually. Peace, for example, starts within each one of us. When we have inner peace, we can be at peace with those around us. When our community is in a state of peace, it can share that peace with neighboring communities, and so on. When we feel love and kindness towards others, it not only makes others feel loved and cared for, but it helps us also to develop inner happiness and peace. And there are ways in which we can consciously work to develop feelings of love and kindness. For some of us, the most effective way to do so is through religious practice. For others it may be non-religious practices. What is important is that we each make a sincere effort to take our responsibility for each other and for the natural environment we live in seriously.

I am very encouraged by the developments which are taking place around us. After the young people of many countries, particularly in northern Europe, have repeatedly called for an end to the dangerous destruction of the environment which was being conducted in the name of economic development, the world's political leaders are now starting to take meaningful steps to address this problem. The report to the United Nations Secretary General by the World Commission on the Environment and Development (the Brundtland report) was an important step in educating governments on the urgency of the issue. Serious efforts to bring peace to war-torn zones and to implement the right to self-determination of some peoples have resulted in the withdrawal of Soviet troops from Afghanistan and the establishment of independent Namibia. Through persistent non-violent popular efforts dramatic changes, bringing many countries closer to real democracy, have occurred in many places, from Manila in the Philippines to Berlin in East Germany. With the Cold War era apparently drawing to a close, people everywhere live with renewed hope. Sadly, the courageous efforts of the Chinese people to bring similar change to their country was brutally crushed last June. But their efforts too are a source of hope. The military might has not extinguished the desire for freedom and the determination of the Chinese people to achieve it. I particularly admire the fact that these young people who have been taught that power flows from the barrel of the gun, chose, instead, to use non-violence as their weapon.

APPENDIX

What these positive changes indicate is that reason, courage, determination, and the inextinguishable desire for freedom, can ultimately win. In the struggle between forces of war, violence and oppression on the one hand, and peace, reason and freedom in the other, the latter are gaining the upper hand. This realization fills us Tibetans with hope that some day we too will once again be free.

The awarding of the Nobel Prize to me, a simple monk from far away Tibet, here in Norway, also fills us Tibetans with hope. It means that, despite the fact that we have not drawn attention to our plight by means of violence, we have not been forgotten. It also means that the values we cherish, in particular our respect for all forms of life and the belief in the power of truth, are today recognized and encouraged. It is also a tribute to my mentor, Mahatma Gandhi, whose example is an indication that this sense of universal responsibility is developing. I am deeply touched by the sincere concern shown by so many people in this part of the world for the suffering of the people of Tibet. That is a source of hope not only for us Tibetans, but for all oppressed peoples.

As you know, Tibet has, for forty years, been under foreign occupation. Today, more than a quarter of a million Chinese troops are stationed in Tibet. Some sources estimate the occupation army to be twice this strength. During this time, Tibetans have been deprived of their most basic human rights, including the right to life, movement, speech, worship, only to mention a few. More than one sixth of Tibet's population of six million died as a direct result of the Chinese invasion and occupation. Even before the Cultural Revolution started, many of Tibet's monasteries, temples and historic buildings were destroyed. Almost everything that remained was destroyed during the Cultural Revolution. I do not wish to dwell on this point, which is well documented. What is important to realize, however, is that despite the limited freedom granted after 1979 to rebuild parts of some monasteries, and other such tokens of liberalization, the fundamental human rights of the Tibetan people are still today being systematically violated. In recent months this bad situation has become even worse.

If it were not for our community in exile, so generously sheltered and supported by the Government and people of India, and helped by organizations and individuals from many parts of the world, our nation would today be little more than a shattered remnant of a people. Our culture, religion and national identity would have been effectively eliminated. As it is, we have built schools and monasteries in exile and have created democratic institutions to serve our people and preserve the seeds of our civilization. With this experience, we intend to implement full democracy in a future free Tibet. Thus, as we develop our community in exile on modern lines, we also cherish and preserve our own identity and culture and bring hope to millions of our countrymen and women in Tibet.

The issue of most urgent concern at this time is the massive influx of Chinese settlers into Tibet. Although in the first decades of occupation a considerable number of Chinese were transferred into the eastern parts of Tibet in the Tibetan provinces of Amdo (Chinghai) and Kham (most of which has been annexed by neighboring Chinese provinces) since 1983 an unprecedented number of Chinese have been encouraged by their government to migrate to all parts of Tibet, including central and western Tibet (which the PRC refers to as the so-called Tibet Autonomous Region). Tibetans are rapidly being reduced to an insignificant minority in their own country. This development, which threatens the very survival of the Tibetan nation, its culture and spiritual heritage, can still be stopped and reversed. But this must be done now, before it is too late.

The new cycle of protest and violent repression, which started in Tibet in September of 1987 and culminated in the imposition of martial law in the capital, Lhasa, in March of this year, was in large part a reaction to this tremendous Chinese influx. Information reaching us in exile indicates that the protest marches and other peaceful forms of protest are continuing in Lhasa and a number of other places in Tibet, despite the severe punishment and inhumane treatment given to Tibetans detained for expressing their grievances. The number of Tibetans killed by security forces during the protests in March, and of those who dies in detention afterwards, is not known but is believed to me more than two hundred. Thousands have been detained or arrested and imprisoned, and torture is commonplace.

It was against this background of this worsening situation, and in order to prevent further bloodshed, that I proposed what is generally referred to as the Five Point Peace Plan for the restoration of peace and human rights in Tibet. I elaborated on the plan in a speech in Strasbourg last

APPENDIX

year. I believe the plan provides a reasonable and realistic framework for negotiations with the People's Republic of China. So far, however, China's leaders have been unwilling to respond constructively. The brutal suppression of the Chinese democracy movement in June of this year, however, reinforced my view that any settlement of the Tibetan question will only be meaningful if it is supported by adequate international guarantees.

The Five Point Peace Plan addresses the principal and interrelated issues which I referred to in the first part of this lecture. It calls for

(1) Transformation of the whole of Tibet, including the eastern provinces of Kham and Amdo, into a Zone of *Ahimsa* (non-violence);

(2) Abandonment of China's population transfer policy;

(3) Respect for the Tibetan people's fundamental human rights and democratic freedoms;

(4) Restoration and protection of Tibet's natural environment; and

(5) Commencement of earnest negotiations on the future status of Tibet and of relations between the Tibetan and Chinese peoples. In the Strasbourg address I proposed that Tibet become a fully self-governing democratic political entity.

I would like to take this opportunity to explain the Zone of *Ahimsa* or peace sanctuary concept, which is the central element of the Five Point Peace Plan. I am convinced that it is of great importance not only for Tibet, but for peace and stability in Asia.

It is my dream that the entire Tibetan plateau should become a free refuge where humanity and nature can live in peace and in harmonious balance. It would be a place where people from all over the world could come to seek the true meaning of peace within themselves, away from the tensions and pressures of much of the rest of the world. Tibet could indeed become a creative centre for the promotion and development of peace.

The following are key elements of the proposed Zone of *Ahimsa:*

- The entire Tibetan plateau would be demilitarized;

- The manufacture, testing, and stockpiling of nuclear weapons and other armaments on the Tibetan plateau would be prohibited;

- The Tibetan plateau would be transformed into the world's largest natural park or biosphere. Strict laws would be enforced to protect wildlife and plant life; the exploitation of natural resources would be carefully regulated so as not to damage relevant ecosystems; and a policy of sustainable development would be adopted in populated areas;

- The manufacture and use of nuclear power and other technologies which produce hazardous waste would be prohibited;

- National resources and policy would be directed towards the active promotion of peace and environmental protection. Organizations dedicated to the furtherance of peace and to the protection of all forms of life would find a hospitable home in Tibet;

- The establishment of international and regional organizations for the promotion and protection of human rights would be encouraged in Tibet.

Tibet's altitude and size (the size of the European Community), as well as its unique history and profound spiritual heritage make it ideally suited to fulfill the role of a sanctuary of peace in the strategic heart of Asia. It would also be in keeping with Tibet's historical role as a peaceful Buddhist nation and buffer region separating the Asian continentǐs great and often rival powers.

In order to reduce existing tensions in Asia, the President of the Soviet Union, Mr. Gorbachev, proposed the demilitarization of Soviet-Chinese borders and their transformation into a frontier of peace and good-neighborliness. The Nepal government had earlier proposed that the Himalayan country of Nepal, bordering on Tibet, should become a zone of peace, although that proposal did not include demilitarization of the country.

For the stability and peace of Asia, it is essential to create peace zones to separate the continent's biggest powers and potential adversaries. President Gorbachev's proposal, which also included a complete Soviet troop withdrawal from Mongolia, would help to reduce tension and the potential for confrontation between the Soviet Union and China. A true peace zone must, clearly, also be created to separate the world's two most populous states, China and India.

The establishment of the Zone of *Ahimsa* would require the withdrawal of troops and military installations from Tibet, which would enable India and Nepal also to withdraw troops and military installations from the Himalayan regions bordering Tibet. This would have to be achieved by international agreements. It would be in the best interest of all states of Asia, particularly China and India, as it would enhance their security, while reducing the economic burden of maintaining high troop concentrations in remote areas.

Tibet would not be the first strategic area to be demilitarized. Parts of the Sinai Peninsula, the Egyptian territory separating Israel and Egypt, have been demilitarized for some time. Of course, Costa Rica is the best example of an entirely demilitarized country.

Tibet would also not be the first area to be turned into a natural preserve or biosphere. Many parks have been created throughout the world. Some very strategic areas have been turned into natural "peace parks." Two examples are the La Amistad Park, on the Costa Rica-Panama border and the SiAPaZ project on the Costa Rica-Nicaragua border.

When I visited Costa Rica earlier this year, I saw how a country can develop successfully without an army, to become a stable democracy committed to peace and the protection of the natural environment. This confirmed my belief that my vision of Tibet in the future is a realistic plan, not merely a dream.

Let me end with a personal note of thanks to all of you and our friends who are not here today. The concern and support which you have expressed for the plight of the Tibetans has touched us all greatly, and continues to give us courage to struggle for freedom and justice; not through the use of arms, but with the powerful weapons of truth and determination. I know that I speak on behalf of all the people of Tibet when I thank you and ask you not to forget Tibet at this critical time in our country's history. We too hope to contribute to the development of a more peaceful, more humane and more beautiful world. A future free Tibet will seek to help those in need throughout the world, to protect nature, and to promote peace. I believe that our Tibetan ability to combine spiritual qualities with a realistic and practical attitude enables us to make a special contribution, in however modest a way. This is my hope and prayer.

In conclusion, let me share with you a short prayer which gives me great inspiration and determination:

For as long as space endure,
And for as long as living beings remain,
Until then may I, too, abide
To dispel the misery of the world.

Thank you

APPENDIX

HIS HOLINESS THE DALAI LAMA'S VISION FOR A FREE TIBET

The following is the official translation of The Guidelines for Future Tibet's Polity and Basic Features of Its Constitution. His Holiness the Dalai Lama issued this document on February 26, 1992. In it, His Holiness makes some very important suggestions for making future Tibet a modern democracy. He categorically declares that he will not hold an official position in the government of future Tibet.

INTRODUCTION

Although it is difficult to predict future, all human beings who wish to achieve happiness and avoid suffering must plan for future. As a result of the Chinese occupation, Tibetans in Tibet are deprived of their basic human rights; this tragic situation cannot be permitted to continue for long.

Tibet has a recorded history of over 2,000 years, and according to archaeological findings, a civilization dating back to over 4,000 years. In terms of geographical features of the country, as well as in terms of race, culture, language, dress and customs, Tibet is a distinct nation.

Under Tibet's Kings and the Dalai Lamas, we had a political system that was firmly rooted in our spiritual values. As a result, peace and happiness prevailed in Tibet.

However, by the middle of this century, Chinese occupation forces marched into Tibet through its eastern border regions of Kham and Amdo. Soon after, the Chinese intensified their military repression in Tibet, driving our political situation to a crisis point. In the face of this, I had no alternative, but to comply to my people's request to assume full responsibility as the head of state of Tibet, although I was then only 16.

In the hope of winning peace and happiness for my people, I tried for years to establish an amicable relationship with the powerful and authoritarian Chinese officials. Also, I set out to reform the unsavory aspects of our social system. With the view to introducing democracy, I constituted a committee consisting of some 50 members. On the recommendation of the committee, some social welfare reforms were implemented, but my efforts towards introducing further reforms failed as the Chinese had by then converted Tibet into their colony.

As soon as the Chinese army had gained full control of Tibet, they shed their initial semblance of discipline and politeness to become ever more demanding and repressive. Brutal forces were used to suppress the Tibetan resistance, first in Kham and Amdo, and finally in the whole of Tibet by March 1959.

As a result, I was compelled to seek refuge in India in order to continue our struggle for the cause of Tibet. Among my initiatives in exile were to see to it that the Tibetan refugees, who were arriving in India in thousands, were given proper education and rehabilitation facilities. I also set out to continue my earlier plans to democratize Tibetan society.

In 1960, the first representative form of government, through the Assembly of Tibetan People's Deputies (the Tibetan legislative body), was introduced in India. Since then we have had eleven such Assemblies. In 1961, I promulgated a constitution for future, free Tibet, based on the principles of modern democracy. In general, this Constitution received overwhelming support from the Tibetans. The Tibetans, however, strongly opposed one provision, which stipulated that if circumstances demanded, the power of the Dalai Lama could be taken away according to the Constitution. Therefore, this provision had to be revised.

In 1963, an even more comprehensive draft constitution was announced. In an attempt to democratize the exile Tibetan Administration, the Assembly of Tibetan People's Deputies was entrusted with the authority to abolish the traditional bipolar system of appointing monk and lay officials to each position. The Assembly also annulled all the hereditary titles and prerogatives granted to small groups of people under the old system. In its place, new guidelines were introduced by which government officials would be appointed in a democratic fashion.

The 1963 draft constitution also authorized a Council of Regents to assume the powers of the Dalai Lama under specific circumstances if that was seen to be in the highest interest of the nation. In deference to the wishes of the people, as I stated earlier, and circumstances prevailing at that time, the constitution gave the ultimate authority of the government to the Dalai Lama. Naturally, I was not satisfied with this clause. I felt that this constitution fell far short of my aim for a genuine democracy.

APPENDIX

Therefore, in my speech of the March 10 Anniversary in 1969, I declared that when the Tibetans regained their right to rule themselves, the people must decide for themselves as to what kind of system of government they wanted. I also stated that it was not certain whether the system of government with the Dalai Lama as the supreme head would continue or not.

About three decades have passed since the draft constitution of 1963 was promulgated. During those years, the world has changed dramatically and people throughout the world have begun to value democratic rights more than ever before. They have realized that democracy is the foundation for the free expression of human thoughts and potentials. Therefore, Tibet also must change when it becomes free.

With regard to the question of Tibet, although it is an international issue, the Chinese leadership has failed to respond positively to my overtures of 1987 and 1988. This is unfortunate, because I undertook these two initiatives as sincere and timely efforts to find a peaceful solution to the issue of Tibet.

The issue of Tibet is not merely a question of the survival of a people with their own distinct history and culture, it also has direct bearing on the fate of this world and Asian peace, and particularly upon the relationship between the world's two most populous nations: India and China. At stake is also the serious question of human rights, as enshrined in the United Nations Universal Declaration of Human Rights, and the world body's efforts to put an end to the era of colonialism and expansionism. Even the Chinese people themselves are opposed to the present Chinese system of governance and are demanding changes.

Chinese dissidents in exile have come to realize and accept the reality that Tibet and China are two completely separate entities. They have also come to recognize the fact that the Tibetans have the right to independence and self-determination. They find no justification in their leadership's claim that Tibet is a part of China.

Globally speaking, the values of democracy, freedom and justice are being appreciated and accepted more widely, especially in Eastern European countries where the totalitarian system, labeled centralized democracy, is giving way to a true and free democracy. The peoples of these nations are now gaining freedom and independence from oppressive regimes.

Similarly, the Tibetan Administration and population in exile, and more especially the Tibetans in Tibet, are striving hard for our freedom. For over 40 years, our brethren in Tibet have lived under an oppressive and tyrannical regime, completely deprived of basic human rights. Naturally, 99 percent of them—be they young, old, cadres, officials—are deeply resentful of the Chinese occupation of Tibet.

Despite the tremendous risks involved, many young people in Tibet have chosen to sacrifice their personal interests to demonstrate against Chinese rule in Tibet. Today there is much better understanding of the Tibetan issue in the world and this has heightened international interest in, and support for, our cause. In the light of this, the Chinese leadership will have no alternative but to abandon its rigid policy and come to the negotiating table to find a peaceful solution to the question of Tibet. It will not be long before the Chinese rulers find themselves compelled to leave Tibet.

When this joyful occasion comes, the time when the Tibetans in Tibet and those in exile are re-united in a free Tibet, the present totalitarian system, dubbed centralized democracy, will have to give way to true democracy under which the people of all the three provinces of Tibet, namely U-Tsang, Kham and Amdo, can enjoy the freedom of thought, expression, and movement. My hope is that Tibet will then be a zone of peace, with environmental protection as its official policy. I also hope that Tibetan democracy will derive its inspiration from the Buddhist principles of compassion, justice and equality.

I believe that in future, Tibet should have a multi-party system of parliament, and that it should have three organs of government— legislature, executive and judiciary—with a clear separation of powers between them, each independent of the other and vested with equal powers and authority. As I have often said, Tibet belongs to Tibetans, and especially to those who are in Tibet. Therefore, Tibetans in Tibet shall bear the main responsibility in future Tibet's democratic govern- ment. Moreover, Tibetan officials presently serving the government of Chinese-occupied Tibet should bear even greater responsibility as they have more experience in running the affairs of the state. It is important that such Tibetan officials eschew all feelings of uncertainty and doubt. Instead, they should strengthen their determination to improve the quality of the future administration of Tibet, and re-dedicate themselves to the cause of Tibetan freedom.

Of course, some Tibetans, egged on by their Chinese masters, have said and done detrimental things. They have done this either due to ignorance or out of fear. Therefore, I see that no purpose will be served by seeking retribution for their past deeds. What is vitally important is to strive unitedly for a happy future.

Personally, I have made up my mind that I will not play any role in the future government of Tibet, let alone seek the Dalai Lama's traditional political position in the government.

There are important reasons why I have made this decision. There is no doubt that Tibetans, both in and outside Tibet, have great hope in, and reverence for, me. From my side too, I am determined to do whatever I can for the well-being of my people. The fact that I am in a position to do this is due to my karma and prayers over past lives. However, in future I will not hold any official position in the government. I will most likely remain a public figure who may be called on to offer advice or resolve some particularly significant and difficult problems which could not be overcome by the existing government or political mechanisms. I think I will be in a better position to serve the people as an individual outside the government.

Moreover, if Tibet is to survive as an equal member of the modern international community, it should reflect the collective potential of all its citizens, and not rely on one individual. In other words, people must be actively involved in charting their own political and social destiny.

It is, therefore, in the interests of the Tibetan people, both long- and short-term, that I have come to this decision, and not because I am losing interest in my responsibilities. There is no need to worry on this count.

Once Tibet regains its freedom and the Chinese forces are withdrawn, there will be a transitional period before the adoption of a new constitution. During this period the existing Administration in Tibet, with all its Tibetan functionaries, will be retained to look after such affairs of State, such as health, economy, education, culture, and transport and communications. This means the Tibetan officials presently working under the Chinese should be ready to assume full responsibilities.

The interim government will be headed by a president, who will assume all the political powers presently held by me. The present Tibetan Government-in-Exile will be considered dissolved ipso facto. Although no one will be entitled to special privileges by virtue of his/her position in the Tibetan Administration in exile, I hope the officials of the exile Administration will willingly accept whatever responsibilities are entrusted to them in view of their qualifications, experience and abilities.

The principal responsibility of the transitional government will be to form a Constituent Assembly with representatives from all parts of Tibet. The Constituent Assembly, in turn, will prepare Tibet's new constitution on the basis of various drafts prepared in exile. This new constitution will be adopted only with the assent of the interim President. Then, in accordance with the constitution, the interim President will appoint an Election Commission, which will conduct the election of the new government.

PROVISIONAL ORDER DURING THE TRANSITIONAL PERIOD

The time between the withdrawal of repressive Chinese forces from Tibet and the formation of a new Tibetan government, elected in accordance with the democratic constitution, shall be referred to as the "transitional period."

1. Since we must have an interim President to head the government during the transitional period, the following procedures will be followed to appoint him or her.

   a) I shall constitute a small committee of leaders from Cholka-Sum, or the three provinces of Tibet. This committee, in consultation with the officials of various departments throughout Tibet, will summon an emergency meeting of all the deputies representing administrative divisions no smaller than a district.

   The meeting, in turn, will elect not more than seven candidates, from whom I shall appoint one as the President.

b) In the event of this meeting failing to elect the candidates, I shall directly appoint the interim President.

2. The interim President, whether appointed directly or from the elected candidates, will take the oath of office in my presence.

3. Upon taking the oath of office, the interim President will be vested with all the powers and responsibilities of government hitherto entrusted to me.

4. The interim President will form a Constituent Assembly. Within one year of its formation, the Constituent Assembly will finalize the new Constitution of Tibet, after studying the draft proposals.

5. The interim President will appoint the Chairperson and other members of the Election Commission. In accordance with the newly-adopted constitution, the Election Commission will conduct the election of members of the Tibetan legislative bodies, their chairpersons, as well as the President and the Prime Minister.

6. The entire process—from the date of adoption of the Constitution to the election of legislative members and the President and the formation of the government—should not exceed two years.

7. The Constituent Assembly of Tibet shall comprise of not less than 250 representatives elected from cities, towns, regions, districts, etc.

8. The first task of the Constituent Assembly will be to establish the rules on the basis of which it will conduct its proceedings.

9. The Constituent Assembly will be deemed to have ceased to exist as soon as the new parliament is sworn in.

10. Likewise, the interim President, and the Election Commission appointed by him will relinquish their positions as soon as the new Assembly is sworn in. From then on, the business of a representative form of government will begin in accordance with the Constitution.

The preparation of comprehensive draft constitutions for several alternative models of democracy is underway at the moment. However, the Constituent Assembly, comprising of representatives from all regions of Tibet, will have a final say in deciding which form of constitution should be adopted. What I have done here is to give a preliminary picture of what to expect in future Tibet's democratic set-up.

PRINCIPAL FEATURES OF THE CONSTITUTION

Salient Features: The Constitution of Tibet will be the supreme law and source of all political powers in Tibet.

Nature of Polity: The Tibetan polity should be founded on spiritual values and must uphold the interests of Tibet, its neighbouring countries and the world at large. Based on the principles of Ahimsa, and aimed at making Tibet a zone of peace, it should uphold the ideals of freedom, social welfare, democracy, cooperation and environmental protection.

Fundamental Principles of the Government: The Tibetan Government will observe and adhere to the United Nations Universal Declaration of Human Rights, and promote the moral and material welfare of its citizens.

Renunciation of Violence and Military Force: Tibet will be a zone of peace, based on the principles of nonviolence, compassion and protection of the natural environment. Tibet will remain non-aligned in the international communities and will not resort to war for any reason.

APPENDIX

Fundamental Rights: All Tibetan citizens will be equal before the law. They are entitled to equal rights without discrimination on grounds of sex, race, language, religion, social origin, etc.

Other Fundamental Rights: All Tibetan citizens will have the right to life, liberty and property; and freedom of speech and expression, freedom to form associations, to publish and disseminate news and views. They will have the right to be gainfully employed, whether in the government or in any institution or department under its authority.

Right to Vote and Hold Public Office: All citizens of Tibet, men or women, will have the right to hold public office and vote in accordance with the law.

Ownership of Land: For the benefit of the people and their habitat, the lands within the territory of Tibet shall be distributed appropriately according to the nature of the land. The distribution of lands will be for the purpose of residence, farming, buildings, factories, business and other livelihood purposes. Lands not privately owned will remain with the state.

The Economic System: Avoiding the two extremes of capitalism and socialism, Tibet will formulate a special economic system to suit its own needs. The taxation system of Tibet will be based on income criteria.

Education and Culture: Since education is key to the development of good human beings and to ensuring social progress, special attention will be paid to formulate a sound educational policy. All assistance will be given to schools, universities, institutes for science, technology and other professional trainings.

Public Health: A public health care system will be established in order to provide adequate health care facilities to the people.

Legislative Power: The legislative power of the Tibetan Government will be vested in the two chambers, namely the House of Regions and the

House of People. Bills passed by them must receive President's assent before becoming law. The House of People will be the highest law-making body. It will consist of representatives directly elected by citizens from all constituencies, which will be demarcated in accordance with population distribution. The House of Regions will consist of members elected by the assemblies at regional level. A limited number of members (the number to be specified in the Constitution) in this House will be nominated by the President.

Executive Power:

a) If the parliamentary system of government is adopted, there shall be a President and a Vice President elected by members of the two national-level Houses and regional assemblies.

b) The executive power of the government, under the parliamentary system, will rest with the Prime Minister and the Council of Ministers formed by the Prime Minister. The Prime Minister must be from a party or any other group constituting majority of members present in the House of People. Failing this, all the members of the House of People will elect the Prime Minister.

Judicial Power: For the purpose of interpreting and upholding the Constitution, as well as for ensuring impartial adjudication of cases involving the State or individuals, there will be a judicial organ which is independent of the other two organs, legislative and executive, of the government. There will be a Supreme Court, which is the highest judicial and appellate court of justice.

Regions: The Tibetan National Assembly will decide the demarcation of Tibet's regions after taking into account the regional economic, geographical, demographic, and transport and communications features. In each region, there should be an assembly consisting of members elected by the people of the particular region. This assembly will be the regional legislative organ.

Also, every region will have a Governor appointed by the President, and a Cabinet headed by a chief Regional Minister, who in turn, is elected by the regional assembly. All the judicial power in the region will be vested in a regional High Court.

In view of the local needs, the regional assemblies can pass laws and regulations affecting their respective regions. Except for some very important matters, the regional assemblies will have the full authority to make decisions governing their respective areas of jurisdiction.

This is an example of one model of parliamentary system. There are various other models of parliamentary or non-parliamentary democracies. A draft constitution based on each of these models is being prepared in consultation with legal experts so that the future Constituent Assembly can choose the one that is seen to be most suitable to Tibet. It is not for me to make this decision.

CONCLUSION

Known as the Roof of the World, Tibet is in the heartland of Asia between India and China. The people of Tibet are by nature honest, gentle and kind.

Future Tibet will be a peace-loving nation, adhering to the principle of Ahimsa. It will have a democratic system of government committed to preserving a clean, healthy and beautiful environment. Tibet will be a completely demilitarized nation.

Although technological advancement has brought material prosperity to much of today's world, it has also resulted in the loss of respect for human beings. Human beings have also lost much of their freedom, so much so that they have become the slaves of machines. While a privileged few live in an island of plenty, the vast majority has to go without even the most basic necessities of life.

In order to prevent this kind of economic disparity, a more preferable economic course needs to be charted for future, free Tibet. Although we will go for a free economy, our economic policy will be aimed at serving the interest of the nation and general masses. We will make efforts to ensure that all the citizens are able to get the basic necessities of life.

In our international policy, Tibet will not align itself with the policy and ideology of any other nation. It will remain neutral in the true sense of the word. Tibet will maintain harmonious relations with its neighbours, based on equality and mutual benefit. It will renounce hostility and promote friendly relations with all nations.

I hope all sincere and right-thinking Tibetans will strive with a sense of pride and joy to attain the goals I have stated in the foregoing lines.

THE DALAI LAMA

CHRONOLOGY & TIMELINE

Sixth century B.C.	Buddhism founded by Siddhartha Gautama (the Buddha)
Seventh century A.D.	Reign of King Songtsen Gampo
Eighth century A.D.	Reign of King Trisong Dretsen
1391	Birth of First Dalai Lama
1475	Birth of Second Dalai Lama
1543	Birth of Third Dalai Lama
1571	Third Dalai Lama visits Mongolia
1589	Birth of Fourth Dalai Lama in Mongolia
1617	Birth of Great Fifth Dalai Lama

1912
Tibet declared
independent

Sixth century B.C.
Siddhartha Gautama
founds Buddhism

500 BC AD 1900 1925

1933
Thirteenth
Dalai Lama Dies

1935
Birth of Fourteenth
Dalai Lama (Tenzin Gyatso)

1642	Great Fifth becomes spiritual and political head of Tibet
1645	Great Fifth begins construction of Potala Palace
1683	Sixth Dalai Lama is born
1708	Birth of Seventh Dalai Lama
1758	Birth of Eighth Dalai Lama
1805–1875	Rule by four short-lived Dalai Lamas
1876	Birth of Great Thirteenth Dalai Lama; Chefoo Convention between Great Britain and China
1903	Invasion of Tibet by British

1950
Chinese invasion of Tibet

1959
Dalai Lama
flees to India

1950   1975   2000

1989
Dalai Lama wins
Nobel Peace Prize

CHRONOLOGY

1912	Thirteenth Dalai Lama declares independence of Tibet
1935	Birth of Fourteenth Dalai Lama
1950	China invades Tibet and takes control of country
1959	Dalai Lama flees to India
1960	Dalai Lama sets up Tibetan government in exile
1967	Dalai Lama visits Japan and Thailand
1973	Dalai Lama travels to Europe
1979	Dalai Lama tours United States; sends fact-finding team to Tibet
1988	Dalai Lama proposes "middle way" for Tibet
1989	Dalai Lama wins Nobel Peace Prize
1990s	Two hundred thousand Tibetans exiled from Tibet by Chinese
2001	Dalai Lama reiterates peaceful approach to Tibetan problems

NOTES

CHAPTER 1:
The Fourteenth Dalai Lama

1 Claude B. Levenson, *The Early Life of the Dalai Lama Tenzin Gyatso.* Berkeley, CA: North Atlantic Books, 2002, p. 14.
2 Ibid., p. 7.
3 Roger Hicks and Ngakpa Chogyam, *Great Ocean: An Authorized Biography of the Buddhist Monk Tenzin Gyatso, His Holiness the Fourteenth Dalai Lama.* London: Penguin Books, 1990, p. 59.
4 Ibid., p. 61.

CHAPTER 2:
History of the Dalai Lamas

5 Glenn H. Mullin, *The Fourteen Dalai Lamas.* Santa Fe: Clear Light Publishers, 2001, p. 40.
6 Ibid., p. 45.
7 Ibid., p. 59.
8 Ibid., p. 91.
9 Ibid., pp. 167, 169.

CHAPTER 3:
Triumph and Turmoil

10 Glenn H. Mullin, *The Fourteen Dalai Lamas.* Santa Fe: Clear Light Publishers, 2001, p. 256.
11 Ibid., p. 255.
12 Roger Hicks and Ngakpa Chogyam, *Great Ocean: An Authorized Biography of the Buddhist Monk Tenzin Gyatso: His Holiness the Fourteenth Dalai Lama.* London: Penguin Books, 1990, p. 41.
13 Ibid., p. 42.

CHAPTER 4: Buddhism

14 Tenzin Gyatso, the Fourteenth Dalai Lama, *The World of Tibetan Buddhism.* Boston: Wisdom Publications, 1995, p. 65.
15 Kevin Trainor, ed., *Buddhism: The Illustrated Guide.* New York: Oxford University Press, 2001, p. 64.
16 Ibid., p. 68.
17 Tenzin Gyatso, the Fourteenth Dalai Lama, *How to Practice: The Way to a Meaningful Life.* New York: Pocket Books, 2002.

18 *The World of Tibetan Buddhism,* p. 59.
19 Trainor, p. 92.
20 Ibid., p. 170.
21 Tenzin Gyatso, *Freedom in Exile: The Autobiography of the Dalai Lama.* New York: HarperCollins, 1990, pp. 33–34.

CHAPTER 5: Tenzin Gyatso

22 Tenzin Gyatso, *Freedom in Exile: The Autobiography of the Dalai Lama.* New York: HarperCollins, 1990, p. 21.
23 Ibid., p. 18.
24 Ibid., p. 29.
25 Claude B. Levenson, *Tenzin Gyatso, The Early Life of The Dalai Lama.* Berkeley, CA: North Atlantic Books, 2002, p. 77.
26 *Freedom in Exile,* p. 54.
27 Roger Hicks and Ngakpa Chogyam, *Great Ocean: An Authorized Biography of the Buddhist Monk Tenzin Gyatso, His Holiness the Fourteenth Dalai Lama.* London: Penguin Books, 1990, p. 85.
28 *Freedom in Exile,* pp. 98–99.
29 Ibid., p. 128.
30 Hicks and Chogyam, p. 115.

CHAPTER 6: Leader in Exile

31 Tenzin Gyatso, *Freedom in Exile: The Autobiography of the Dalai Lama.* New York: HarperCollins, 1990, p. 145.
32 Ibid., p. 159.
33 Ibid., p. 231.

CHAPTER 7:
Tibet Under Communism

34 Chin-en Wu, "Political Development in Tibet, Fall of 1959 to Fall of 1964," (December 14, 2001). Available online at *http://sitemaker.umich.edu/cewu/files/tibet2.doc.*
35 Boycott China for Tibet, "The Chinese Occupation of Tibet—Issues and Key Dates." Available online at *http://buyhard.fsnet.co.uk/dates.htm.*
36 Warren Smith, Jr., *Tibetan Nation.* Boulder, CO: Westview Press, 1996, p. 561.
37 FDCH Congressional Testimony, Senate Foreign Relations Committee, June 13, 2000.

NOTES

CHAPTER 8:
Citizen of the World

38 Warren Smith, Jr., *Tibetan Nation*. Boulder, CO: Westview Press, 1996, p. 623.

39 *Vital Speeches of the Day*, August 15, 1996, Vol. 62, Issue 21, p. 642.

40 *Vital Speeches of the Day*, May 1, 1997, Vol. 63, Issue 14, p. 423.

41 Ibid.

42 FDCH Congressional Testimony, Senate Foreign Relations Committee, June 13, 2000.

43 *Vital Speeches of the Day*, May 1, 2001, Vol. 63, Issue 14, p. 438.

44 Lewis Simons, "Tibetans Moving Forward Holding On," *National Geographic*, April 2002.

CHAPTER 9:
Thoughts of the Dalai Lama

45 Bryan Doyle, *Commonweal*, June 15, 2001, p. 9.

46 Tenzin Gyatso, the Fourteenth Dalai Lama, *Awakening the Mind, Lightening the Heart: Core Teachings of Tibetan Buddhism*. San Francisco: HarperCollins, 1995, p. xiv.

47 Ibid., p. 1.

48 Ibid., p. 12.

49 Ibid., pp. 65–66.

50 Available online at The Sacred Land Initiative, *http://www.sacredland.net/budhistory.htm*.

51 Tenzin Gyatso, the Fourteenth Dalai Lama, *Ethics for the New Millennium*. New York: Penguin Putnam, 1999, p. 4.

52 Ibid., p. 23.

53 Ibid., pp. 71, 73.

54 Ibid., p. 120.

CHAPTER 10:
Roles of the Dalai Lama

55 Tenzin Gyatso, the Fourteenth Dalai Lama. *How to Practice: The Way to a Meaningful Life*. New York: Pocket Books, 2002, p. 12.

ambans—Chinese ambassadors in Tibet

dharma—Basic priniciples of existence in the universe

dhukha—The First Noble Truth of Buddhism: all life involves suffering

guru—Spiritual teacher

karma—Actions that produce consequences

khatas—White scarves offered to lamas as symbols of respect

lama—Buddhist monk and teacher

mantra—Word or phrase spoken over and over during meditation

monastery—Home of monks

nirvana—State of enlightenment

reincarnation—Being reborn in the body of another person

samsara—Constant cycle of death and rebirth

stupa—Buddhist shrine

sutra—Buddhist teaching

tantras—Secret writings of the Buddha

tulku—Enlightened lama who is reborn through the ages

BIBLIOGRAPHY

BOOKS

Gyatso, Tenzin, the Fourteenth Dalai Lama. *Awakening the Mind, Lightening the Heart.* HarperCollins, 1995.

———. *Ethics for the New Millennium.* Penguin Putnam, 1999.

———. *Freedom in Exile: The Autobiography of the Dalai Lama.* HarperCollins, 1990.

———. *How to Practice: The Way to a Meaningful Life.* Pocket Books, 2002.

———. *The World of Tibetan Buddhism.* Wisdom Publications, 1995.

Harrer, Heinrich. *Seven Years in Tibet.* G. P. Putnam's Sons, 1981.

Hicks, Roger, and Ngakoa Chogyam. *Great Ocean: An Authorized Biography of the Buddhist Monk Tenzin Gyatso, His Holiness the Fourteenth Dalai Lama.* Penguin Books, 1990.

Levenson, Claude B. *Tenzin Gyatso: The Early Life of the Dalai Lama.* North Atlantic Books, 2002.

Mullin, Glenn H. *The Fourteen Dalai Lamas.* Clear Light Publishers, 2001.

Pandell, Karen. *Learning From the Dalai Lama: Secrets of the Wheel of Time.* Dutton, 1995.

Penney, Sue. *Buddhism.* Heinemann, 2001.

Smith, Warren Jr. *Tibetan Nation.* Westview Press, 1996.

Snelling, John. *Buddhism.* The Bookwright Press, 1986.

Trainor, Kevin, ed. *Buddhism: The Illustrated Guide.* Oxford University Press, 2001.

Tsering, Diki. *Dalai Lama, My Son.* Penguin Putnam, 2000.

Whitney, Stewart. *The Fourteenth Dalai Lama: Spiritual Leader of Tibet.* Lerner Publications, 1996.

OTHER RESOURCES

Boycott China for Tibet. "The Chinese Occupation of Tibet—Issues and Key Dates." Available online at *http://buyhard.fsnet.co.uk/dates.htm.*

Chin-en Wu. "Political Development in Tibet, Fall of 1959 to Fall of 1964." Available online at *http://sitemaker.umich.edu/cewu/files/tibet2.doc.*

Doyle, Brian. *Commonweal.* June 15, 2001.

FDCH Congressional Testimony, Senate Foreign Relations Committee, June 13, 2000.

The Sacred Land Initiative. Available online at *http://www.sacredland.net/budhistory.htm.*

Simons, Lewis. "Tibetans Moving Forward Holding On." *National Geographic.* April 2002.

Vital Speeches of the Day, August 15, 1996, Vol. 62, Issue 21.

————. May 1, 1997, Vol. 63, Issue14.

FURTHER READING

PRIMARY SOURCES

Gyatso, Tenzin, the Fourteenth Dalai Lama. *Awakening the Mind, Lightening the Heart.* HarperCollins, 1995.

———. *Ethics for the New Millennium.* Penguin Putnam, 1999.

———. *Freedom in Exile: The Autobiography of the Dalai Lama.* HarperCollins, 1990.

———. *How to Practice: The Way to a Meaningful Life.* Pocket Books, 2002.

———. *The World of Tibetan Buddhism.* Wisdom Publications, 1995.

Harrer, Heinrich. *Seven Years in Tibet.* G. P. Putnam's Sons, 1981.

Tsering, Diki. *Dalai Lama, My Son.* Penguin Putnam, 2000.

SECONDARY SOURCES

Alldritt, Leslie D. *Buddhism.* Chelsea House Publishers, 2004.

Hicks, Roger, and Ngakoa Chogyam. *Great Ocean: An Authorized Biography of the Buddhist Monk Tenzin Gyatso, His Holiness the Fourteenth Dalai Lama.* Penguin Books, 1990.

Levenson, Claude B. *Tenzin Gyatso: The Early Life of the Dalai Lama.* North Atlantic Books, 2002.

Mullin, Glenn H. *The Fourteen Dalai Lamas.* Clear Light Publishers, 2001.

Pandell, Karen. *Learning From the Dalai Lama: Secrets of the Wheel of Time.* Dutton, 1995.

Penney, Sue. *Buddhism.* Heinemann, 2001.

Smith, Warren Jr. *Tibetan Nation.* Westview Press, 1996.

Trainor, Kevin, ed. *Buddhism: The Illustrated Guide.* Oxford University Press, 2001.

WEBSITES

"The Dalai Lama: A Spiritual Leader in Exile." *CNN.com*

http://www.cnn.com/SPECIALS/2001/dalai.lama/

Biographical information about the exiled Tibetan leader, with numerous links to sites with data on Tibetan and Buddhist-related news.

The Dalai Lama of Tibet

http://www.dalailama.com/

The official site of Tenzin Gyatso, the Fourteenth Dalai Lama.

The 14th Dalai Lama

http://www.nobel.se/peace/laureates/1989/lama-bio.html

Biography of the Dalai Lama created by the Nobel e-Museum; contains text of his Nobel address and other speeches.

Tibetan Government in Exile

http://www.tibet.com/

The official of the Dalai Lama's government in exile, headquartered in India.

TibetNet

http://www.tibet.net/hhdl/eng/

Contains biographical information about the Dalai Lama as well as Tibetan news and history.

INDEX

abbots, 45-46
  See also monasteries
Abhidhamma Pitaka, 36-37
Ah, 3
alms, 38
Altan Khan, 14
ambans, 20, 22
Amdo Province, 3
anger, Dalai Lama on, 83
aristocrats
  and China, 51
  estates of, 5, 46
  and food for Chinese soldiers,
    49-50
army, for Tibet, 29, 40-41, 53
Arsalan Khan, 15-16
assembly, in India, 57
Avalokiteshvara, 35, 78
awakening mind, Dalai Lama on,
  79-80
*Awakening the Mind, Lightening the
  Heart: Core Teachings of Tibetan
  Buddhism* (Dalai Lama), 76

bells, 37
Bhutan, Tibetans fleeing to, 73
bodhichitta, 35
Bodhisattva, 49
bodhisattvas, 35, 78
Bomdila, India, 56
Brugpa School, 11
Buddha. *See* Siddhartha Gautama
Buddharupas, 37
Buddhas, 35
Buddhism, 30-41
  and Buddhas, 35
  and calendar, 44-45
  and China, 51-52
  and compassion, 34, 35, 76, 77,
    78, 79
  and Dalai Lama, 40-41, 86-87
  and death, 79. *See also* reincarna-
    tion
  and deities, 35

and *dharma,* 31-32, 43, 79
and festivals, 39-40, 44-45, 47
founding of, 9
and Four Noble Truths, 32-33
and good acts, 32, 38-39
and India, 59
and Japan, 59
and *karma,* 32, 33, 34, 38
and Kublai Khan, 10
leaders of. *See* Dalai Lamas
and love, 78, 79
and meditation, 34, 36, 37, 78-79,
  80
and middle-way approach, 72
and monasteries in India, 59
and Mongols, 14
and morality, 33-34
and *nirvana,* 32, 33, 35, 37, 77,
  78, 79, 80
and Noble Eightfold Path, 33-35,
  37, 38-39, 47
and poems, 76, 77
and reincarnation, 32, 35
schools of, 11, 35, 40
and shrines in homes, 37-38
and Siddhartha Gautama
  (Buddha), 9, 31, 32, 36, 37,
  39, 40, 72, 77, 79, 80
and Songtsen Gampo, 9
teachings of, 31-32, 77
and temple, 37
and Thailand, 59
and thoughts of Dalai Lama,
  75-84
and Tibet under Chinese rule,
  64, 65, 66-67, 68, 69, 71, 74, 86
Tibetan, 35, 40-41
and understanding life, 79
and wisdom, 34-35
and worship, 35-38.
See also Dalai Lamas; Fourteenth
  Dalai Lama (Tenzin Gyatso)
Bush, George H.W., 71
butter candles, 37

INDEX

INDEX

Theravada Buddhism, 35, 59

Third Dalai Lama, 13-14, 15

Third Noble Truth, 33

Thirteenth Dalai Lama, 3, 4-5, 26-29, 41

"Three Baskets," 36

Three Jewels of Buddhism, 43, 76, 78

Thupten Gyatso, 26.
   See also Thirteenth Dalai Lama

Tibet
   and army, 29, 40-41, 53
   and Buddhism, 35, 40-41
   and Chinese influence, 26
   and civil war (1600s), 15-16
   Dalai Lama's vision of free, 124-134
   and earthquake of 1950, 46
   and empire, 9
   farming in, 5, 46
   first maps of, 17
   and foods, 5
   geography of, 3
   and Great Britain, 25-27
   and Gurkha invasion, 23
   and independence, 29
   and invasion by Chinese warlord, 27-29
   and Manchus, 22-24
   and Mongols, 10, 14-16, 20-22
   and Russia, 25-27
   and social classes, 45-46
   as theocracy, 3, 29.
   See also Tibet, China's invasion and control of

Tibet Autonomous Region (TAR), 65

Tibet, China's invasion and control of, 46-54, 55-61, 62-69
   and Buddhism, 64-65, 66-67, 68, 69, 71, 74, 86
   and Chinese settlers in Tibet, 73, 74
   and collectivization, 51, 63-64, 65, 66

and conditions inside Tibet, 73
and Cultural Revolution, 65, 66
and deaths of Tibetans, 65, 68, 73, 86
and education of children, 60-61, 66
and elections, 65
and execution of freedom fighters, 68
and fact-finding teams to Tibet, 60-61, 63, 66
and family, 64-65
and food for Chinese soldiers, 49-50, 64, 65
and food shortages, 49-50, 65-66
and human rights violations, 60, 65, 67, 68, 86, 109-113
and invasion of Tibet, 46-48
and modernization of Tibet, 74
and prison and labor camps, 65
and release of Panchen Lama from prison, 59-60
and Tibet as totalitarian society, 73-74

Tibetan resistance to, 50, 67, 68, 69

Tibetan revolts against, 51-53, 56, 58-59, 65-66

and Tibetans fleeing to India, Nepal, and Bhutan, 56-59, 73, 86

Tibetan Children's Village, 58

Tibetan People's Congress, 65

Tripitaka, 36-37

Trisong Dretsen, 9-10

tsampa, 5

Tsangyang Gyatso, 20
   See also Sixth Dalai Lama

Tsewang Rabten, 22

Tsongkhapa the Great, 11

tulkus, 35

Twelfth Dalai Lama, 24-25

United Nations, and China's takeover of Tibet, 47

PICTURE CREDITS

RICHARD WORTH has thirty years' experience as a writer, trainer, and video producer. He has written more than twenty-five books, including *The Four Levers of Corporate Change*, a best-selling business book. Many of his books are for young adults on topics that include family living, foreign affairs, biography, history, and the criminal justice system.

MARTIN E. MARTY is an ordained minister in the Evangelical Lutheran Church and the Fairfax M. Cone Distinguished Service Professor Emeritus at the University of Chicago Divinity School, where he taught for thirty-five years. Marty has served as president of the American Academy of Religion, the American Society of Church History, and the American Catholic Historical Association, and was also a member of two U.S. presidential commissions. He is currently Senior Regent at St. Olaf College in Northfield, Minnesota. Marty has written more than fifty books, including the three-volume *Modern American Religion* (University of Chicago Press). His book *Righteous Empire* was a recipient of the National Book Award.